ADVANCED AVIATION
MODELLING

D1560742

ADVANCED AVIATION MODELLING

JOHN McILLMURRAY

THE CROWOOD PRESS

First published in 2005 by
The Crowood Press Ltd
Ramsbury, Marlborough
Wiltshire SN8 2HR

www.crowood.com

British Library Cataloguing-in-Publication Data
A catalogue record for this book is available from the British Library.

ISBN 1 86126 753 3

Photographs on page 2:
TOP: One of the great attractions of modelling Luftwaffe types – plenty of colour. The model is a Revell 1/72 Fw 190A-8 backdated to an A-5, and has numerous features associated with modelling that is a little more advanced than what comes straight out of the box.

BOTTOM: Typical of advanced modelling, this Hasegawa 1/72 Tornado GR 1 has had its wings and weapons replaced with the excellent polyurethane wing set from Airwaves and polyurethane and photo-etched weapons from Flightpath. The model also sports after-market decals and a lot of pastel work.

Typeset by Textype Typesetters, Cambridge

Printed and bound in Singapore by Craft Print International Ltd

Contents

Acknowledgements

This book is dedicated to my mum, who sadly died whilst it was being written.

Special thanks are due to:

My dear wife Sandra for all her encouragement and patience and for all the times she has said, 'Yes dear, it's lovely . . . what is it?'

IPMS Farnborough for their motivation and advice, especially Rod Ulrich and Alan Simpson.

My good friend Andrew Eaton, for his support and dedicated friendship and for taking me on my first trip to the Hannants shop in Colindale, London, and to the IPMS Nationals/Scale Modelworld show every year since 1995. Thanks are due him also for his considerable help with this book, especially the last chapter.

Martin Hale for his considerable help in the box on 'Wood Effect' and the box on 'Rigging'.

The Daylight Company for the provision of one of their excellent lamps.

The Small Shop EU for providing the delightful little Hold & Fold tool.

Airbrush UK for their very generous provision of the excellent Iwata airbrush and compressor.

Torway for their provision of the 1/72 Academy F-15E (modelled as an IAF F-15D in this book).

Humbrol for the provision of the 1/48 Mosquito NF.30.

The Hobby Company for the provision of the Tamiya 1/72 Spitfire Mk V (modelled as a Mk II in this book).

Aeroclub for providing the 1/48 de Havilland Gipsy Moth kit, as well as a great selection of Contrail and other products. Thanks also to John Adams in person who has always made himself available to help me.

David Hannant for generously supplying a goodly number of paints as well as the 1/48 Aires Super Detail cockpit set for the Mosquito, and the Cutting Edge control surfaces, also for the 1/48 Mosquito.

MDC for providing their whole range of 1/32 Bf 109 detail sets, the Finnish decals sheet, as well as the Gunze Sanyo Mr Surfacer products.

Foreword

By Richard Franks (former editor of Scale Aviation Modeller)

When I was asked to write this Foreword by John McIllmurray I must say that I was delighted. I have both worked with John in my position as editor of Scale Aviation Modeller and have known him on a personal level for a number of years now. John's experience as a modeller is typical of most, in that he started at an early age making kits purchased from a local shop, and then over the years drifted away from the hobby before returning to it again once all the other aspects of adult life had been resolved. This is the route most modellers will take. We usually begin by building plastic construction kits as children, but gradually other interests and 'growing up' take away from both the time and enthusiasm available to give to the hobby. Later, the vast majority will return, once they reach an age at which they are settled and have disposable income to support a hobby.

Most of those who return to the hobby will find that it has changed a great deal in the intervening years. Crowood's initial title, Scale Aircraft Modelling by Mark Stanton, offers a sound basis for modellers returning to the hobby and should form the foundations on which you, as a modeller, can start to enjoy the hobby once again. This second book, although entitled Advanced Aviation Modelling, is best thought of as a second-level development in the processes that you will apply during modelling. John has only been back in the hobby for a few years, but in that time he has actively sought to develop areas of modelling that most modellers simply do not have the nerve to venture into. This experience made him an ideal choice to write this book, as he has done everything by both learning from others and by hands-on experience. Such knowledge is priceless in any pursuit, so John's words should assist many of you to get more from this hobby.

Most of us learn our hobbies by practical experience and don't actively seek to become a better modeller – you simply learn how to deal with your mistakes! You become better by applying a series of processes during each stage of model-making that allows you to ensure a set standard. These standards are determined by your experience and we all find ourselves developing a personal style. However, once the basic aspects of model-making have been mastered, it is easy to find yourself very quickly in a rut. At this point, most modellers find themselves wanting more, often fuelled by what you see at model shows and in magazines, as you think 'I wish I could do that . . .'. Learning the processes that allow you to step up the quality of your modelling has always been difficult. Our hobby is very personal and hands-on, so it does not lend itself to easy forms of promoting higher skills. Many of you will be members of a local model club, and for those of you who are not, I urge you to join one. Talking with other modellers is a great way of learning new techniques. Most modellers are willing to share their knowledge, but you are still left with the gap between the spoken word and actually doing it. This new title from John works to fill that gap by showing you via clear narrative and photographs how every aspect of static scale aviation modelling can be developed.

In buying this title, you have already identified that you are looking to develop new skills, and this book has been created in such a way as to promote each aspect of the modelling process. You will need to have a sound basis in model-making already, because you will need to understand many of the terms and processes that are taken for granted within these pages. As John takes you through each aspect of modelling you will soon see how all of these become one process, and your modelling will improve as a result. They will all need practice and many of them will take a great deal of time to perfect. But as you progress, you need to remember that this is a hobby and as such must remain relaxing. As a male-dominated pastime there is an aspect of competitiveness about it, but that does not mean you need to lose sight of what it is all about, relaxation. Many hobbies can also be frustrating, and modelling is no different. If it was not complex it would not be a hobby, as relaxation is actually best achieved by focusing on a set subject and engrossing yourself in it. Modelling can take up a lot of time, but never let it become a chore, something you 'must' do, because then the enjoyment will be gone. Maintaining a sensible outlook is the key; the more pressure you apply to yourself to achieve, the less you will enjoy what you are doing.

The urge to reproduce something in miniature goes back thousands of years. It has always been based within the love of a particular subject and the desire to create a tangible version of it in miniature. I believe John's work here should act as an incentive to many of you to develop new skills that will add a new dimension to your hobby. Of course, there will be certain aspects of these skills that you may not wish even to consider, but everything is here for those of you that do. I am sure that in reading this book many of you will see the processes that go into achieving certain results and will think 'Ahh, so that's how they do it.' That is what *Advanced Aviation Modelling* is all about.

Richard A. Franks

Preface

We all have our own story that makes up who and what we are. I was born into a British Armed Forces family in West Germany, as it was then, in 1971. I cannot remember how old I was, but I recall picking up a red plastic Airfix Gnat from our local NAAFI. The only other thing I remember was that the kit was in a bag! When the film *Star Wars* came out in 1977, my friends and I wanted to make the sci-fi models that were becoming available, and then in 1980 when the whole of West Germany seemed to become one big military exercise area as *Crusader 80* kicked off, we all started making Tamiya tanks. The tank thing has never really left me and certainly was the only area of the hobby I was interested in when I myself joined the Army for five years.

The next modelling chapter of my life came in my final year at Theological College when my wife decided I needed a hobby for a bit of escapism and proceeded to go out and buy me a Tamiya Mini Cooper! Sandra has continued to encourage me in this area ever since and as long as the models aren't too big or dirty looking, she is happy. Perhaps the greatest turning point in my modelling life came in December 1994 whilst ministering in the Aldershot area. It was at this juncture that my local model shop introduced me to the International Plastic Modelling Society (IPMS) club held at Farnborough, at which I was exposed to a great variety of modelling interests and skills. It was here that I began asking question after question about the 'hows' and 'whys' of the finished model on the table. I still ask questions – I need

to! IPMS Farnborough was also my first exposure to the competitive side of the hobby. Entering one's 'effort' into a competition is not everyone's cup of tea and if you are not careful you might end up taking things a bit too seriously, but for me the competitions provide motivation to try to do better next time.

For a number of years now I have found my domestic circumstances (that is to say, stuck at home with ill health) have enabled me to spend time writing modelling articles for various modelling magazines. The time has also been taken to experiment with the production of my own multimedia 1/72 scale update and conversion sets, mostly based on the Ju 88 family, and even to produce a number of Ju 88 complete kits, all under the label AIMS. Being stuck indoors as a young man waiting on operations isn't any fun and so you can imagine how delighted I was when The Crowood Press contacted me about the possibility of doing a book. Certainly the time issue was not a problem, but what about the author? One look at my modelling library and you would note that I am a somewhat limited modeller. I really only do 1/72 scale due to space restrictions, and although I sometimes drool over the detail that comes ready made in larger scales I do actually prefer the smaller scale and have set out on something of a private quest to try to make my own smaller models just as detailed as the larger competition models. But I am not only a limited modeller in terms of scale, but also interest as well. I really hardly ever go near anything other than World War II aircraft; to be perfectly honest, I would be happy spending the rest of my days modelling de Havilland Mosquitoes and Ju 88s! Doing a book with a much wider scope of subject matter has certainly taken me out of my comfort zone, but that is no bad thing – it is when you are out of your comfort zone that you learn the most, and that has also been my experience here.

The title of this book, *Advanced Aviation Modelling*, is not intended to put off the aspiring modeller, merely to indicate that the modelling described herein is beyond the experience of the pure 'kit builder'. I sincerely hope that you will enjoy and be informed by what you read. If you are not, then the fault is most probably my own, but if you are wanting to improve your game then I hope to have been of help, just in the way that the folk at the IPMS clubs at Farnborough and more recently Salisbury have been of help to me. I also want to improve my own game for what it is worth. I would love to be able to scratchbuild like Nicholas Poncini and paint like Geoff Coughlin and one day I hope I will be able to. That is the spirit of *Advanced Aviation Modelling* – learning and improving by modelling outside of your comfort zone!

The author hard at work scratch-building the geodetics of the MPM 1/72 Wellington IC.

Introduction

What progress are you making as a modeller? When I go to the IPMS Nationals or Scale Model World, as it is now known, I come away asking myself that same question. Am I improving? Am I stuck in a rut? Do I knowingly rush and cut corners that I know will be to the detriment of the model? The aim of this book is to commend to you the benefits of trying to get more out of your interest in making scale-model aeroplanes, by looking deeper into the after-market and home-grown possibilities that exist and thus advance in the hobby. Any overlap in subject matter with Mark Stanton's excellent overview of the hobby is not meant in any way to be disingenuous but is rather the natural result of trying to achieve the stated aim of the book. What the book cannot do is refine your manual dexterity or give you artistic perception. This hobby will always be an individual effort where practice will teach you more than a hundred books of this nature. Put another way, this book can inform, inspire and motivate but it can never generate!

Three unfortunate downsides of trying to achieve the aims of this book exist:

- The absolute necessity of bought or borrowed reference material.
- The need for a slightly wider range of tools and materials.
- The considerable regression in your yearly output of completed models due to the extra time and care taken over them.

Reference material can be very expensive, not to mention limiting in that you end up only making a model once you feel confident you have every reference possible! I am very fortunate to belong to two IPMS clubs and to have a number of good friends who feel they can trust me with their precious books. This is one answer. The Internet, your own camera and fairly inexpensive modelling magazines are another, but sometimes you will just have to fork out the money for the book that shows photos of areas your camera will never be allowed or able to see, and thus your reference library has begun!

Good tools are a must in this hobby. They can cost a lot of money and so need to be seen as investments as their value is appreciated more and more as time and projects pass by. Advanced scale-aviation modelling draws upon a number of extra tools (and materials) perhaps unfamiliar to most modellers. These tools and materials, looked at mostly in Chapters 4 and 11, offer more diversity and in a sense independence from what is currently offered by mainstream and cottage-industry suppliers.

As for the time issue, you may have heard the quibble that we live in a 'hobby-rich and time-poor generation'. For many people that I know this is indeed the situation: life is just too busy, be it due to work or family commitments, or to something else. Introducing an aspect to your modelling that is even more time-consuming than how you model at present simply exacerbates the situation! There is really no way around this one. A friend can lend you that large hard-back book that you will never be able to afford but they cannot lend you time in the same way. You just have to come to terms with the simple truth that better models take more time and that you want to build better-looking models. I wish you all the best in this endeavour.

The Fujimi 1/72 Bf 110C showing scratch-built nose-gun bay, photo-etched interior, vac–form canopy and after–market decals. All part of the fun!

Profile of the F-15E modelled in Chapter 1.

CHAPTER 1

Scratchbuilding

Martin Hale's extraordinary 1/48 scratchbuilt Felixstowe F.3 – few of us will ever venture this far.

It just does not seem possible to scratchbuild at this level, but with the right materials, scale plans and bags of patience and skill it obviously is possible!

Scratchbuilding is a great way to get 'back to basics'. It is an aspect of modelling that is rich in reward as you look upon the finished result, and it is all of your own making. Indeed, there is something almost nostalgic in scratchbuilding your own detail and therein is something of the pleasure of this style of model-making. It is almost as if you have been transported back to a time when everything had to be your own work and it really was an achievement to represent something faithfully.

Of course, when we talk of scratchbuilding, this covers a wide range of activity, from making a complete aircraft to adding a missing retraction arm on an undercarriage. Not many of us will ever be in a position or mood to make an entire aircraft, but from time to time we may like to have a go at trying to make a fairly straightforward bulk part. Moulding block is perfect for this, as it can be carved, sanded or sawed very nicely with no grain to worry about. The most difficult task is getting hold of an offcut in the first place. Moulding block is used mainly by prototype modellers for the automobile industry. Some of the larger aftermarket names in our own hobby may be able to help or at least point you in the right direction. Once you have some in your possession it is a case of transposing the various measurements from the plans you have onto the two-dimensional surfaces of the moulding block. If the item you are attempting to manufacture is dependent on being able to fit to other kit parts, then this needs to be taken into consideration as well. Once the length has been drawn on the moulding block and the block cut down to size accordingly, you can then transpose onto each end the cross section of the part you are creating (making sure that they line up correctly at both ends). Thus the width can be ascertained and the basic shape cut from the rest of the block. Sanding can then commence to fine tune the transposed cross-section measurements. It then only remains to add any additional raised or scribed detail into your new aircraft part using the scribing techniques described in Chapter 12 and elsewhere in this book. The above work is hugely enjoyable, but don't be too surprised if within a year of all your hard work the 'big boys' go and bring out a kit of the very subject you struggled to create – thanks, Amtech!

Most of us will be happy at one stage in our lives to attempt scratchbuilding a comparatively simply shaped object like this Ju 88H-1 extended fuselage from an offcut of moulding block.

With the help of redundant kit parts (for example, the kit's wing roots) and some scribed detail, your own manufactured part starts to take on a semi-professional look and you start believing you can actually pull the project off!

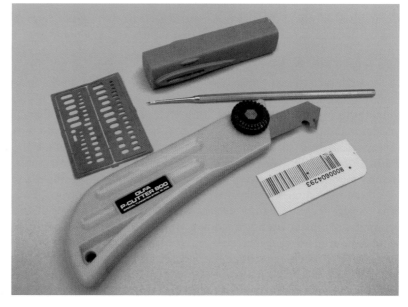

The finished 1/72 Ju 88H-1 project made possible by a bit of moulding block.

The most frequent application of scratchbuilding is in the attempt to model smaller details like the avionics bay in the photograph of this F-15E kindly supplied by the F-15E Strike Eagle.com website. But is it possible?

Yes it is . . . even in 1/72!

For most of us and for the majority of occasions scratchbuilding will be limited to two main categories: that which needs to be done in order to rectify any deficiencies in the kit or aftermarket detail, and that which is superfluous. As far as materials go, the basic rule of thumb is 'if it looks right and it will glue . . . use it'. Every spaceship in a sci-fi film started the same way, with someone looking at a pile of odds and ends and applying their imagination. Most modellers can achieve the results they are after with a selection of wires, styrene sheet, engineering struts, rods and blocks, and of course the good old spares box.

In the first case – scratchbuilding because you need to – you have little choice if you want a fairly accurate-looking model, and that is what advanced scale aircraft modelling is all about. But it is not always that hard to accomplish. For example, none of the 1/72 scale

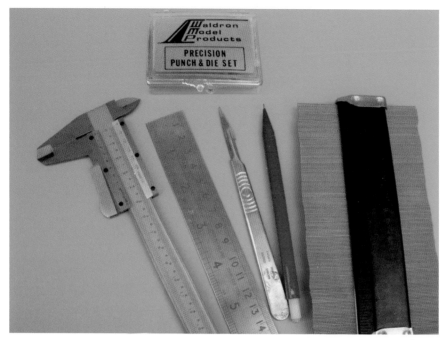

A number of helpful measuring and marking tools will be of use in the process of scratchbuilding. Other tools also come in handy when scratchbuilding, such as the Waldon Precision punch and die set. These tools are very expensive if you are not going to be using them often, but once you have needed them a few times you will be glad that you forked out the expense when you did.

Plastic sheet from Evergreen, pewter sheet, various amperage of electrical wire and Plastruct construction rods in various shapes and sizes from model railway enthusiast shops plus various helpful products by Contrail – sold through people like Aeroclub. All on the right are very helpful materials to have around during scratchbuilding.

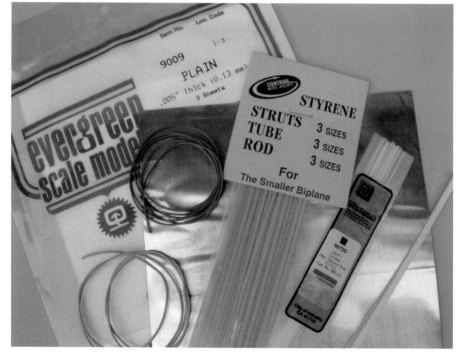

Good tools and the right materials are nothing without good references like those in the Walk Around series by Squadron/Signal and the Modellers' Datafile series by SAM Publications.

Sometimes scratchbuilding using plastic sheet from Evergreen, plastic square rod from Plastruct and a bit of fuse wire can help you to supplement photo-etched brass detail in an effort to represent better the features in a cockpit like this 1/72 Hasegawa F-15E.

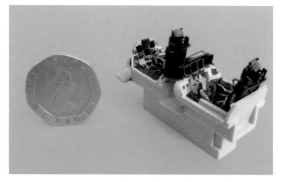

When the model is all painted up you know it looks the way it does because of the extra work you put in to correct it.

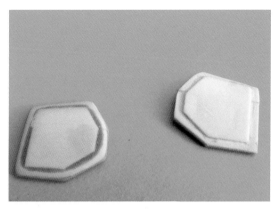

Various thicknesses of Evergreen plastic sheet can be used to create more compound curve items like these F-15E bulged main gear bay doors, which in the kit were flat.

The bulged gear bays are hardly ever on show, but again for the time it took you will be glad you made the effort to remodel them so that they look right; indeed, the majority of scratchbuilding solutions will be for small external problems.

F-15E kits comes with that type's characteristic bulged main gear doors caused by the larger main wheels used on the Strike Eagle. Both Airfix and Hasegawa give earlier style flat main gear doors as separate kit parts, however, making it a relatively easy job to build up your chosen manufacturer's doors by gluing layers of plastic sheet to them in ever decreasing diameters. Filler is then added to the resulting steps in the layers, so that when sanded you end up with a replica of a bulged gear bay door. Sometimes the detail isn't wrong – it is just not there!

SCRATCHBUILDING DETAIL

A lack of detail is not so much in evidence on modern kits, but if they are all you have made you will be perhaps a little shocked when faced with earlier kits or vac-form kits. It is a good exercise to now and then make an older kit or a vac-form kit just for the sake of the extra work involved. In this way, you will be forced to scratchbuild, gaining experience of the discipline, patience and more understanding of the subject at hand. Wheel wells are perhaps the most neglected areas of detail on older kits but simple construction work, with perhaps some cast items taken from a modern kit, can really make a difference and end up far exceeding the detail in newer offerings of the same aircraft type. Have a go! More minor scratchbuilding can be used either to add to kit and brass detail or even to rectify it if need be. In the case of our Hasegawa F-15E, the Eduard photo-etched brass rear console was significantly altered, as was the kit's coaming above it.

It is always more pleasurable, of course, to scratchbuild because you want to, not because you have to. This kind of modelling is usually aimed at detail that would not be on view unless the aircraft in real life was being worked on. These busy-looking models are the real eye-catchers at model shows, and you can end up spending an awful lot of money on every resin and photo-etched brass detail set available to try to be in the running. It is always good to see if you can do some of the work yourself, however. The cost-to-satisfaction ratio is massive, and although the finish might not be as crisp as that which you see in a new resin set by Aires or CMK, it is all your own work and therefore unique.

Start by looking at a photo of what you want to replicate; it is not only essential that you get inspired, but is also helpful if the reference material is comprehensive enough for you to be able to see the essential details you want to model. When you are happy, think about what you are going to cut away. Are you going to be able to use these parts again? Panels are very thin affairs, much thinner than the thickness of

the kit's injection-moulded parts. It is also unavoidable that you will end up with a cutaway part that has decreased in width and height to the value of the thickness and accuracy of your saw cuts! With this in mind, it is a good idea to try to make a replica of the panel by overlaying the kit panel with pewter or the lead foil from wine bottle tops. These materials are strong and capable of being shaped to compound curves, although they cannot carry over any of the kit part's scribed detail (for panels that do show the original scribed detail *see* Chapter 12). Once you are satisfied with the panels you have made, it is

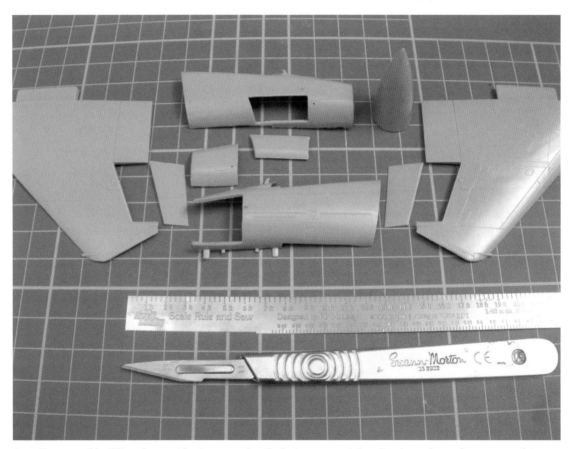

As well as scratchbuilding that rectifies incorrect detail, the same material and tools can be used to open up the model to show off its inner workings. How far you go is up to you and depends upon the extent of the references you have. Work starts with the inevitable surgery, which needs to be done with a razor saw (like the one sold as part of a set by Scale Aircraft Modelling) and a new No. 11 scalpel blade. Much more care should be taken than when surgery is performed in conversion projects as you may not be throwing anything away.

Using a Vernier contour gauge, dividers or just good old dead reckoning and trimming to fit (or all four), the basic construction of the avionics bay is gradually built up with plastic sheet.

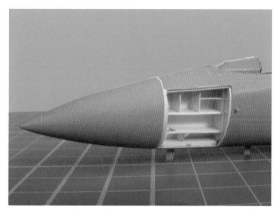

Again using plastic sheet cut to size, the basic detail, in this case the shelving, is cemented in place and left a good while to dry.

Pre-drilled blocks of plastic square rod and anything from the spares box that fits the bill is then cemented in place following the layout given in your references.

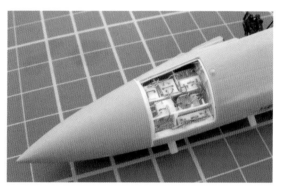

When the stored equipment is firmly set in place various gauges of wire can be superglued into the pre-drilled holes to represent the electrical cabling detail that is sure to be present in abundance.

The same work is carried out on the reverse of the door, and can be made out of resin (see Chapter 11).

The finished scratchbuilt avionics bay is a real achievement and helps the whole model to look 'busy'.

out with the razor saw to remove unwanted kit panels before your scratchbuilding can begin.

The first step is to block in the compartment you are working on. With either a pattern being transposed onto plastic sheet taken from a contour gauge or a few basic measurements from a divider and ruler (and even the curvature of the kit's fuselage if this is exposed and can be placed on some plastic card and drawn around), you can set about cutting out the various bulkheads from plastic styrene sheet. Dry-fitting and tweaking a few times will eventually get you there.

The idea now is gradually to build up the detail as best you can. The majority of equipment will be held in place by various brackets, so shelving has to be added to your boxed-in compartment. Any ribbing visible on the bulkheads can also be added.

It is now time to add your equipment – again, if it looks right, then use it. Boxes are relatively simple items to make from styrene sheet and will look quite good provided that your 90-degree cuts are on the ball. Before adding equipment make sure that any holes which need drilling to help locate cabling and handles are done first; shelving and brackets can be flimsy and will not take much pressure from drilling into items placed on them. Of course, modelling is not quite as straightforward as chapter divisions in a book make it and a certain amount of mingling with other disciplines and materials takes place. In this case, although the equipment in question can be (and was) made purely out of non-specific materials, Reheat do a comprehensive range of photo-etched brass generic radio, radar and instrument faces that are good for this kind of work.

Finally, the wiring and other such detail – low-amp fuse wire is perfect for this and comes in various thicknesses. The wiring used by railway modellers to wire up their points is very fine and is also great for brake piping in 1/72 scale. It is not a good idea to have the wiring all the same amperage, because a more varied array will add contrast and realism. In many ways, all the steps are probably quite true to life and progress quite naturally towards the end objective of having a completed avionics bay. It will also be necessary to add detail to the reverse of the compartment door, however you have made

Sometimes scratchbuilding is necessary because there is just no detail present where there needs to be! Not all kits have the in-depth detail of the modern Tamiya 1/48 Mosquito with its excellent gear bays.

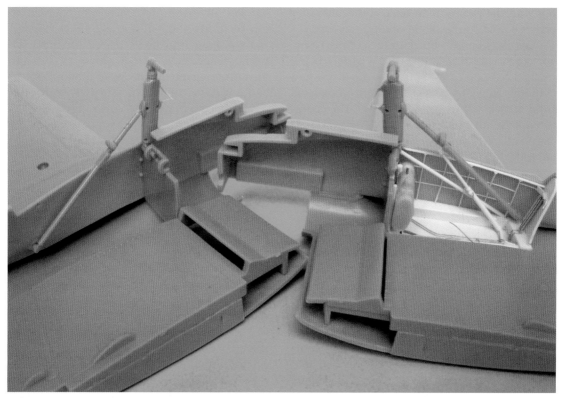

In fact, go back twenty-five years to 1980 and you have an Airfix kit with nothing in the gear bay at all!

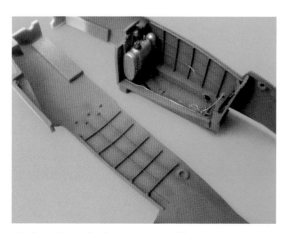

With the help of a few cast copies of kit parts and all the other usual scratchbuilding materials it is an easy enough matter to build up the necessary absent structure – again, good references are necessary.

Much of scratchbuilding relies on the modeller's ingenuity in coming across products or materials and changing their uses to suit the need of the present project. Here the Hair-Coat product designed for just that by the Small Shop EU proves an excellent material for creating fleece covers for ejection seats.

it, as this will no doubt have stiffeners for structural integrity. It may also have wiring depending upon whether or not there are dipoles on the surface.

A passing reference has already been made to the ingenuity of using whatever materials fit the bill in your attempt to scratchbuild detail. A novel way of giving your F-15's Aces II ejection seats some 'fleece' covers is to coat them with Hair-Coat from the Small Shop EU. The product is designed for exactly that – hair and coats, admittedly with military figure modelling in mind, but it looks great as a fleece seat cover as well! Using just a bit more of the setting varnish to mat it down to scale you can produce really lovely results – especially with careful dry-brushing to highlight a small degree of the fur. Another medium for scratchbuilding is Tamiya masking tape, as it has just the right thickness to mimic accurately the external stiffeners like those visible on the leading edges of the F-15's vertical stabilizers, or the front armour and dinghy compartment on a 1/48 Mosquito. Why not even use guitar string, which in 1/48 scale represents the Mosquito's gear door retraction springs very well. Use your imagination to search for the right materials for the job and enjoy the reward of having created detail that is entirely your own workmanship.

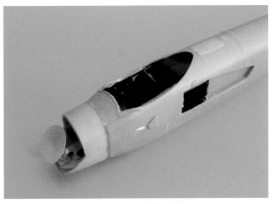

. . . or the frontal armour and dinghy compartment on this Airfix 1/48 De Havilland Mosquito NF.30.

The finished effect looks as it should and with no sign of glue build-up where a plastic alternative may have been difficult to place correctly first time.

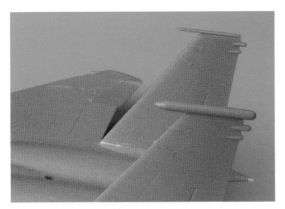

Tamiya masking tape is just thick enough to represent raised detail such as those leading edge stiffeners on the Hasegawa 1/72 F-15E . . .

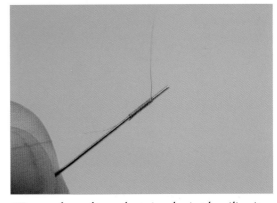

Wire can be used to make springs by simply coiling it around the appropriate gauge of rod.

In this way, small springs like the canopy arrester at the back of the pilot's head armour on this 1/32 Hasegawa Bf 109G-6 can be made without difficulty and with maximum realism.

If you know someone that plays the guitar ask them if they have any spare steel coiled string. This can be utilized to make very realistic-looking springs like those found to the rear of the Mosquito gear bays to keep the gear bay doors from flapping about.

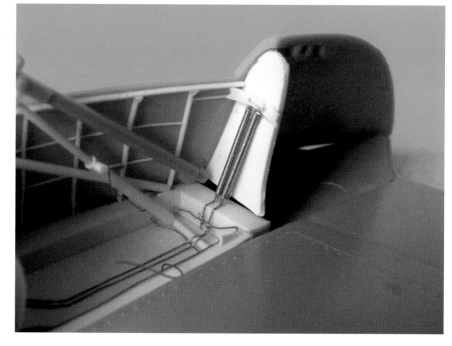

CHAPTER 2

Photo-Etched Brass

In aircraft modelling, no matter what the scale, a number of questions are bound to be asked: What needs adding? What needs replacing? What could I do to make the model a bit different? And finally: Is what I want to do achievable? This chapter looks at the use of photo-etched brass to try to answer some of these questions. Photo-etched brass has been around for some time now, with dozens of aftermarket manufacturers churning out new sets each week. With hundreds of choices available you have to be pretty unlucky to pick an aircraft type that has not been covered by this industry. Photo-etched brass has helped our hobby in many ways, for instance one of the great challenges of modelling 1/72 scale aircraft is how to make them just as detailed as their larger-scale counterparts. Detail found in 1/48 scale aircraft is often absent from smaller scales due to the limitations of the manufacturer's tooling or budget, and when such detail is present it is often over-scale. Photo-etched brass can both remedy the problem of missing detail and significantly reduce the unwanted volume of over-scaled kit detail by replacing it with wafer-thin parts. It is this 'thinness' that commends the use of the medium for another reason – namely the limited amount of reduction in the surrounding plastic needed for such items as cockpit sidewall detail, which can be superglued straight on without making the cockpit aperture look too narrow.

In this chapter we will be using two sets by probably the biggest name in photo-etched detail, Eduard, as well as two sets from a perhaps lesser known but just as good company, Part. Both manufacturers' sets are excellent in quality, comprehensive in detail and easy to use, so long as a few 'house rules' are followed. The benefits of using photo-etched brass parts have already been mentioned, but I hope they will become even clearer during the course of this chapter.

Working with photo-etched brass is not everybody's idea of fun, however, for four reasons. Firstly, superglue (cyanoacrylate) is essential to bond the photo-etched items together as well as to the host aircraft, be it in resin or plastic, and works by creating a fast-setting skin. This can be very unforgiving, and misaligned brass parts can be damaged in the endeavour to remove them. Secondly, cyanoacrylate gives off vapours that can cause very bad

Some of the great names in photo-etched brass designs: Verlinden, Airwaves, Eduard, Extra Tech . . . there are many more!

headaches, even with the window open. Thirdly, regarding the brass items themselves, even with the best tweezers in the world it is almost inevitable that from time to time items will ping into the gaping jaws of the 'carpet monster' to be lost forever! Finally, there is only so much that two-dimensional photo-etched brass detail parts can do, and the larger the scale the more limited this medium becomes when representing parts that have compound curves. Polyurethane resin detail sets cope with such detailed requirements in their stride, but in turn have their own difficulties to be overcome. In the meantime, two-dimensional photo-etched brass detail can be bulked out by layering over with PVA wood glue, or even used as a basic template for making your own three-dimensional part out of plastic sheet.

Despite the difficulties, both the superglue and the tweezers are musts when using brass, as is a brand-new scalpel blade. Brass kinks very

easily and is difficult to tidy up; a 45-degree cut with a new blade significantly reduces this risk. Many brass items are designed to fold up so as to represent three-dimensional detail. This is not the most flattering feature of photo-etched brass as it often leaves horrible join lines, but the work can be done accurately and tidily thanks to the innovation of the Small Shop EU and their 'Hold & Fold' tool. If you have ever wondered how people managed before mobile phones the same applies to photo-etched brass once you own one of these little babies; perfect 90-degree folds every time! Other photo-etched brass parts are designed not to fold but to be layered on top of other photo-etched brass parts to become three-dimensional. Masking the parts together at one end and prising open the other end just enough to add a touch of superglue to the inside of the sandwiched parts can reduce misalignment problems greatly. The procedure is repeated for each new layer.

The beginnings of a great radar build. Note how well the items from the Part set fit the Academy kit they are designed to go with. Note also the wonderful quilt effect behind where the navigator sits. Photo-etched brass handles these small 'intense' areas of flat detail very well . . .

... as may be
attested to by the
finished look of the
radar equipment
used to model this
Academy 1/72
F-15E as an Israeli
Air Force 'D'.

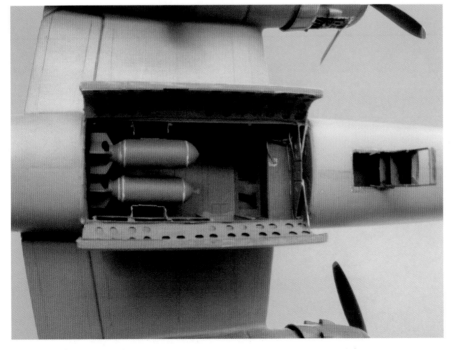

Not only does
photo-etched brass
do justice to small
areas of flat detail,
but it can also be
used to build up an
entire bomb bay.
Here the Eduard set
for the Italeri B-25
shows just that.

THE FINER DETAILS

Still other brass detail is designed to replace existing kit detail, for example grilles. It is here that perhaps photo-etched brass truly comes into its own. As the panels and grilles in real life are flush fitted, so the kit detail needs to be removed in order for the brass items to take its place. A good way of doing this is by drilling them out with a hobby drill. A good transformer that can go down to zero revolutions is a worthwhile purchase here and will minimize unwanted damage. Too high a revolution setting will increase the likelihood of the drill bit 'scatting' on impact with the surface, scarring the plastic and perhaps snapping the drill bit. With the resulting aperture cleaned up, the replacement brass part is dropped into

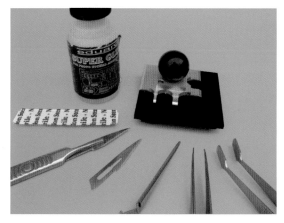

Some very helpful tools for dealing with etched brass, namely Eduard superglue (cyanoacrylate), scalpel blades, a selection of tweezers and the excellent 'Hold & Fold' tool by the Small Shop EU.

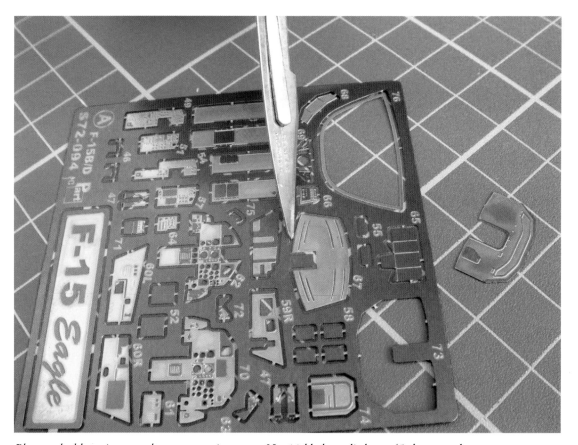

Photo-etched brass items are best cut out using a new No. 11 blade applied at a 45-degree angle.

Some photo-etched brass items have multiple folds included in their design. The Hold & Fold tool is a godsend!

The Hold & Fold tool comes into its own where the parts are hard to hold onto at the same time, such as with these 1/72 FuG 200 radar dipoles by Kora.

It is hard to see how the Kora FuG 200 dipoles could have looked as neat without the use of the Hold & Fold tool.

Care needs to be taken to get the right position where photo-etched brass parts are designed to be layered on top of one another.

Photo-etched brass really comes into its own where grilles are concerned. There is no other way of getting such detail in 1/72.

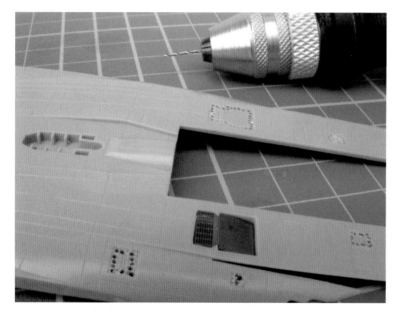

A hobby drill with a good transformer is a very useful tool to have and makes short work of helping cut out the existing grille detail on this Hasegawa 1/72 F-15E so that the etched brass replacement grilles can fit flush on the model.

place. Using Tamiya masking tape, or its equivalent, to bridge the brass part prevents the part falling through and also helps to achieve a flush fit. When you are happy with the fit the best way to secure the part in place is by capillary action. With an old, but clean, blade dipped into a drop of superglue, apply the 'wet' blade to the join line on the reverse face and let capillary action do the rest. Performing this procedure from the reverse side will give a far

neater finish. If, during your preparation for the fitting of the brass grilles, you have been extremely accurate, then a great way to finish off the procedure is to brush around the join lines with some Gunze Sangyo Mr Surfacer. This liquid filler is exceptional and, once dry, sands down very nicely with wet and dry abrasive paper.

The benefits of brass can be appreciated in many different features of a model like the F-15.

With the grilles taped in place to hold them flush with their surroundings superglue can be run into the join from the reverse side with an older scalpel blade. Any superglue that runs out onto the surface of the model can be easily cleaned up with wet and dry abrasive paper.

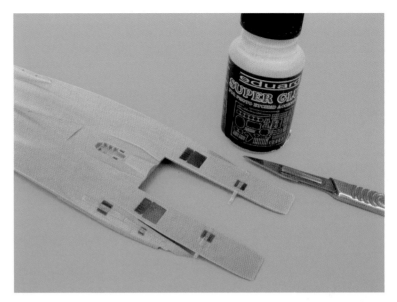

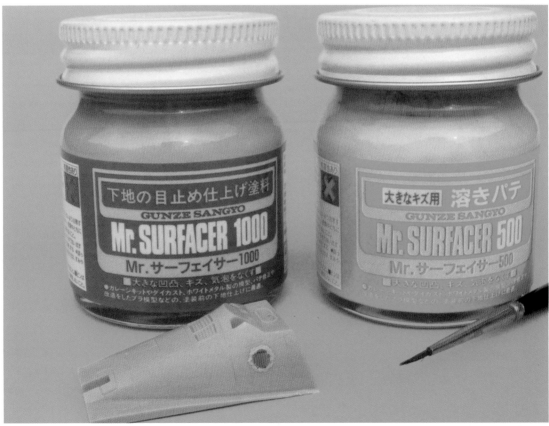

Gunze Sangyo Mr Surfacer products are excellent micro fillers, perfect for tidying up around photo-etched brass grilles.

For instance, the Academy F-15E offering relies on decals applied to featureless surfaces in the cockpit. This is fine if the canopy is to be closed, but not if you really want to be able to see raised detail. Such detail has been provided by Part through their UK distributor, Aeroclub. Many sets are on offer but the decision was made to model an F-15D and so that set was chosen. The difference is dramatic indeed and shows just how comprehensive modern photo-etched brass sets have become. As mentioned previously, there is only so much a kit manufacturer can do and in 1/72 scale such fine detail as missile canards and fins, ordnance shackles, engine actuators, perforated undercarriage arms and radar equipment will always look better as photo-etched brass items.

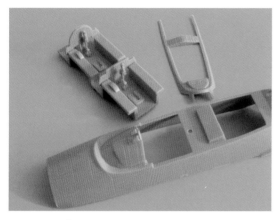

The rather two-dimensional Academy F-15 'office'. Many kits rely on decals to give the necessary details in the cockpit, but this is hardly good enough even in 1/72 if you want the hood open.

The photo-etched brass answer from Part is quite breathtaking and certainly provides ample justification for using this medium. There are some seventy individual parts in this photo!

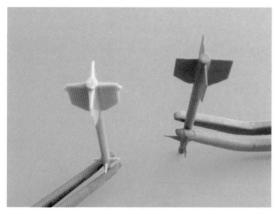

When it comes to such wafer-thin items as the canards of missiles, even the best manufacturers are restricted by what injection moulding can and cannot do. Photo-etched brass provides the answer to the problem of scale in this area . . .

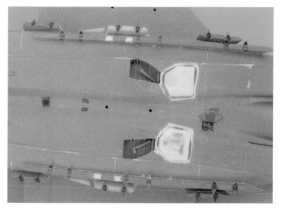

. . . as it does with all other items that are just too slender in real life to be adequately represented by any other medium. Here the Hasegawa 1/72 F-15E (with homemade and Academy F-15E pylons) is decked out with twenty-four individual ordnance shackles, each with four individual folds.

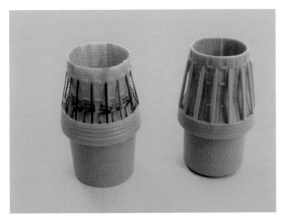

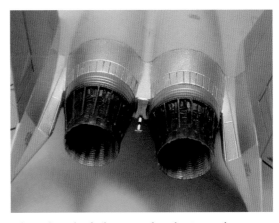

The benefits of photo-etched brass are beyond question in this case – the exhaust actuator detail has been replaced with brass items on the Hasegawa F-15E part and is standing next to the same part but by Academy (the Hasegawa original kit actuators fared no better, by the way).

The end result of what seemed at the time to be an endless amount of fiddly brass items to add. Such detail really needs to be done in brass where 1/72 is concerned.

With the help of photo-etched brass and other techniques, such as scratchbuilding, undercarriage legs can be made to look like they really could work. Here the excellent items from the Part set come in for praise once again as they help to super-detail the Academy F-15 that was to end up as an Israeli Air Force 'D' (see Chapter 5).

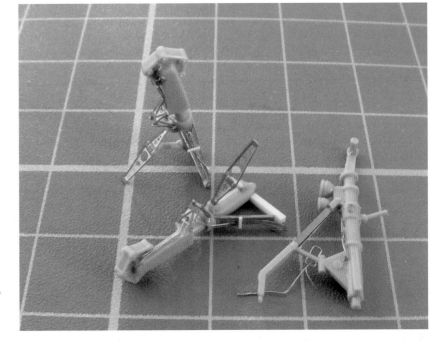

CHAPTER 3

Polyurethane Resin

Having looked at scratchbuilding and photo-etched brass in the previous two chapters as media for detailing scale aircraft, let us now look at the third great medium available – polyurethane resin. Many of the big names in the aftermarket area of this hobby specialize in multi-media sets, with the majority of the parts being exquisitely detailed resin items. Other companies use resin predominantly for bulk structural parts, mainly for conversion projects (*see* Chapter 9). In both cases the resin products are almost exclusively designed to replace injection-moulded kit parts completely. To that end the medium is far less fiddly than photo-etched brass, as all the fine detail is already attached, but working with resin has its own sets of problems as well as advantages.

The key problems faced when working with resin concern health and safety and the need for 'surgery'. Due to the casting procedure the majority of resin parts will come with what is called a 'casting block'. This block is needed for all the air to be evacuated into during casting in a de-gassing chamber. Removing the casting block, either with a saw or a hobby drill sanding attachment, creates fine particles of

Some of the great names in Polyurethane resin super-detail sets are Aires, Verlinden, CMK (Czech Master's Kits) and MDC (Model Design Construction). These companies have some great master modellers working for them. It is something of a mystery as to how these people get the cast parts they produce out of the silicone moulds without wrecking them.

Resin engine sets like those produced by Aires are excellent and a bit of extra scratchbuilding to the surrounding kit areas makes for an atmospheric or 'busy' look. Here the old Italeri 1/72 B-25 has been super-detailed with the help of some resin Wright R-2600s.

Aires not only produce great resin engines but more involved super-detail sets as well. Here the Aires super-detail set, comprising engine, engine covers and cockpit, has brought to life the little 1/72 Hasegawa Bf 109G-14 in the markings of Eric Hartmann.

As if a full engine and cockpit build were not enough, Aires went even further in their super-detail set for the Tamiya 1/72 Spitfire Mk I by including a full complement of Browning 0.303in machine guns with bays and photo-etched brass covers.

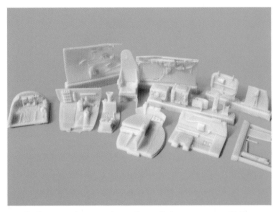

Both the quantity and quality of the contents of these sets seem to just get better and better, here is the resin cockpit components of the Aires 1/48 de Havilland Mosquito Mk VI detail set – exquisite!

Only resin can depict such fine details as the cooling holes on these Aires 0.50in calibre machine guns – and these are 1/72!

polyurethane resin that then become airborne – and these airborne particles are toxic! A mask should always be worn and a wet cloth used to wipe up debris from the workbench; also note that you really don't want to be doing this kind of work near children or food. The other difficulty in using resin is in regard to the amount of surgery required. This is quite an obvious point to make, considering that we

have already noted that one of the key features of this medium is its use to replace kit parts or detail, but nevertheless it is a difficulty.

This difficulty is never more apparent than in the area of the cockpit. Injection-moulded kits have cockpit walls that are too thick for scale. Layering resin detail directly on top, as you might get away with when using photo-etched brass, simply compounds the situation.

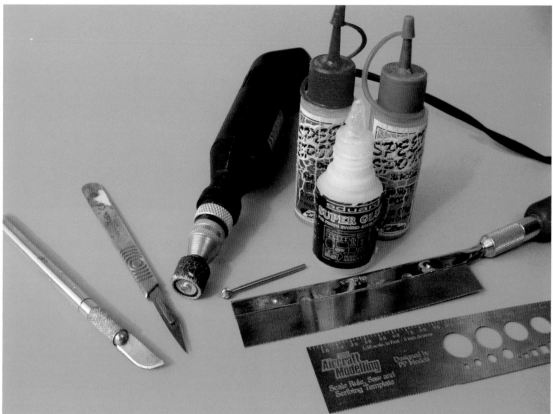

A number of different tools are extremely helpful when using resin detail or conversion sets, for example a No. 11 Swann-Morton blade for fine separation work and a No. 10 rounded blade by X-Acto for scraping. Glues such as Speed Epoxy and Eduard superglue are obviously needed for cementing resin together with other similar or dissimilar materials. Various saws are most valuable for both removing large cast blocks and for finer work. Finally, as many resin sets are designed to super-detail cockpits and other internal areas, a good hobby drill with various cutting and sanding attachments is recommended. Be sure to wear a dust mask if using these sanding attachments on resin parts as the polyurethane dust is toxic.

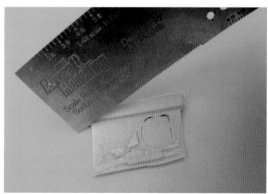

Resin is a very brittle material to work with and detail parts need to be separated from their casting blocks with care.

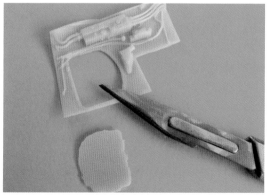

Where a razor saw cannot go a sharp No. 11 blade can, repeated shallow passes being preferred over deep pressure cuts.

The only appropriate means of action is to reduce the thickness of the injection-moulded cockpit walls as much as you dare by initially using a cutting attachment on a hobby drill. The cutting attachment will make short work of reducing the bulk of the plastic to be removed, but the transformer must not be set too high nor the cutting attachment applied to one spot for too long. Ignoring this rule will almost certainly result in the plastic melting under the friction, causing unhelpful distortions on the outer surface of the model. Various hobby chisels and grades of wet and dry paper will help to complete the uniformity of the work. The aim is to be able to see daylight shining through the thinned-out plastic – not work for the faint-hearted.

Of course, the smaller the scale the harder it

Numerous types of cutting burr and sanding attachments exist for hobby drills such as those produced by Hobbycraft and Dremel. As long as you are careful, short work can be made of thinning out the plastic from the innards of a model aircraft's cockpit area . . .

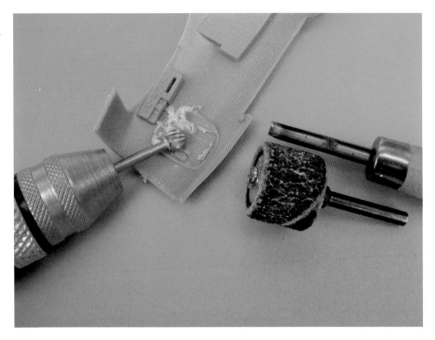

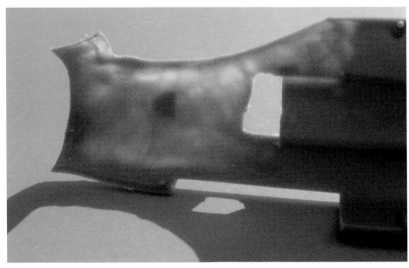

. . . until it looks like this.

One of the most rewarding stages of working with these wonderfully detailed resin sets is seeing them come to life during the painting process. Every depression in a leather seat cushion and every dial on a radio can be picked out (see MDC Bf 109G-6 cockpit set in Chapter 4).

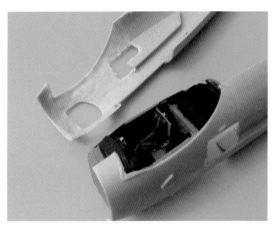

Time to see if you reduced the plastic from inside the kit's cockpit walls enough.

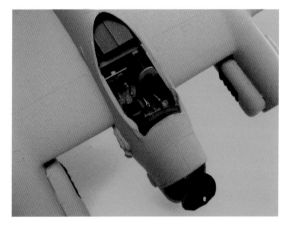

Even with the inside walls of the kit and the reverse of the resin sidewalls thinned as much as you dare, it is very difficult to get the right scale of thickness when using resin sidewall detail. The problem is somewhat exacerbated by using a vac-form canopy, as the material is so thin it doesn't do much to hide the overly thick walls.

is to achieve realistically thin cockpit sidewalls that use resin detail – the reverse also being true. The injection-moulded cockpit area of a 1/32 kit will almost certainly be the same thickness as its 1/72 counterpart, and the same is true for the backing detail of the resin sidewall. Thus the whole problem is distributed over a larger, less noticeable area. One further difficulty involves how to attach polyurethane parts to injection-moulded plastic. As with

In 1/72 the problem is at its greatest, although more could have been done to help my Octopus 1/72 Tigercat with Pavla resin detail I must admit!

photo-etched brass, the resin medium does not 'melt' to bond with plastic but has to be 'grafted' on. Superglue is therefore used to create a fast-setting artificial skin once you are absolutely certain you have everything in the right position, although four-minute epoxy glue is far more forgiving and allows time for 'tweaking'. Both glues rely on the same bonding principles, so it is just a case of determining which glue is most suitable for the job in hand.

The key attraction of working with polyurethane resin detail sets is in their three-dimensional detail. Unlike photo-etched brass, the resin medium can cope with compound curves and even massive undercuts if the mould is two-part; the resin has a great deal of viscosity and the degassing chamber has sufficient pressure. All this adds up to a highly detailed cast part which when painted will bring the whole cockpit to life (*see* Chapter 5).

The majority of modern high detail resin sets are designed for modern kits, the detail of which is so superb that it almost seems sacrilege to take the cutting burr to it! There is, of course, nothing to stop you doing so, but it has already been pointed out that modelling older

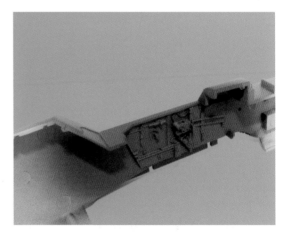

In 1/32 the problem is virtually unnoticeable, especially on a subject like this Hasegawa Bf 109G-6, which has a very convenient sidewall ledge under which the slightly thinned-out resin wall detail sits.

kits is good experience, and so why not see if the resin detail set designed for a modern kit will fit easily enough into an older kit? In the majority of cases it will: the cutting burr that needs to be used anyway for old or new will make sure of that! The extra detail will be far more appreciable on the older kit than on the new, and the existing superb detail on the modern kit can always be supplemented with scratchbuilt detail. Please note that the conformity of old and new cockpit areas which allows the above work to be carried out does not always correspond to the rest of the aircraft. Aftermarket resin replacement control surfaces exist for many models, but sometimes using them for a brand name other than that which they were designed for shows up serious discrepancies in the scale plans that the manufacturers have used to produce their kit. Going ahead and using them will mean extra unlooked for construction work to remedy the discrepancy.

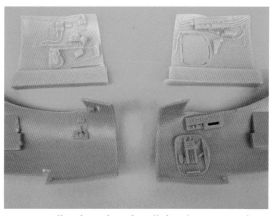

. . . especially where the sidewall detail is concerned.

It is not always necessary to use the kit that the super-detail resin set is designed to go with. Indeed, most sets are designed to go with modern kits, whose detail is already very good; more benefit might therefore come from using the resin set with an older kit that is in more need of the extra detail. In saying that, placing the assembled Aires resin cockpit next to the assembled Airfix 1/48 de Havilland Mosquito cockpit shows just how good this kit was for a 1980 vintage tooling. Nevertheless, the resin set has the upper hand and will benefit the Airfix kit much more than the new Tamiya Mosquito kits available . . .

Although the principle of using modern resin replacement parts on kits other than that recommended is usually trouble free, it is best to be careful before you go chopping off bits of kit.
Here we see a resin replacement rudder by Cutting Edge designed to go with a Tamiya kit revealing quite a noticeable difference between the Airfix and Tamiya renderings of the Mosquito vertical stabilizer and rudder.

CHAPTER 4

Clear Parts

One significant factor in creating a more realistic model involves taking a decision to favour the use of clear vac-form parts over their injection-moulded cousins whenever possible, especially in the smaller scales where the distortions created by even the best injection-moulded parts are at their greatest. A thick, dull or distorted canopy can ruin an otherwise excellent model, and the reverse is equally true. The decision is not an easy one, as you are choosing to favour a medium that is very unforgiving of damage and cannot be sanded or polished. However, with a little extra care and time your model can be finished with excellent transparent parts.

For a good number of years the master model-maker Tore Martin of Falcon Industries has been at the forefront of clear vac-form production. His work is sold in boxed sets or as individual items under the Squadron/Signal Crystal Clear Range and is responsible for enthusing many modellers to make models for which vac-form clear parts are available. But what happens if a clear vac-form part isn't on the market? You must either wait and hope that it soon will be or do something about it yourself! This chapter explains the procedure for making your own clear vac-form parts, but also looks at other areas of clear part modelling that play a vital role in determining the quality of the finished model.

DIY VAC-FORM MODELLING

A small vacuum chamber, a bag-less vacuum cleaner, a toaster, two pairs of pliers or mole

The leading light in vac-form canopies, Falcon Industries based in New Zealand.

There is just no other way of representing aircraft types, like this Grumman Avenger with its various folding and sliding canopy parts open, other than by using vac-form canopies like those produced by Falcon for this Hasegawa 1/72 kit.

grips and a sheet of butyrate are all that are needed to create your own vac-form clear part. It may sound a lot, but you are likely to have most of the items already and butyrate can be bought at many hobby stores or from Squadron/Signal. The main item is obviously the vacuum chamber. A local metalsmith would no doubt be able to help, but the chamber used in this book is nothing more than a cruciform of aluminium folded up like a carton with a lip folded inwards to support a strip of draft excluder tape. A hole just big enough to take an offcut of an old vacuum cleaner attachment has been cut into one side and the hose secured with silicone. The four folds in the metal case have been layered over with extra aluminium and sealed. All that is then needed is some stiff mesh the same size as the aperture and some way of holding a sheet of butyrate firmly in place. In our case, the butyrate is cut to size before being sandwiched in-between two aluminium frames which are then screwed together.

Airfix have recently re-released their 1980 de Havilland Mosquito FB VI as an NF.30. One of the decal options is for a Belgian Air Force machine, one of twenty-four war surplus NF.30s sold to that country post-war. Photographs clearly showed that like many other post-war NF.30s the paint had either been removed or just not applied to the clear perspex nose protecting the H2S radar from prying eyes. That takes care of the motivation; it is now just a case of preparing the kit part representing the perspex area, which needs to be carefully removed from the rest of the nose using a razor saw and brand new scalpel blade. With the kit part cemented together, dental putty can be pushed up into the cavity, making sure to give the part more height by leaving surplus putty at the base. With the part now being a little more robust, thanks to it no longer being hollow, sanding can commence. This sanding is important when taking a vac-form of a 'male' master, as the resulting clear vac-form part will be about 0.5mm wider and taller than the original. Thus the corresponding amount needs to be taken away uniformly from

A simple homemade vacuum chamber on which to make DIY vac-form canopies.

Acetate will just go dull when heated up, so you need to use butyrate, such as that supplied by Squadron/Signal.

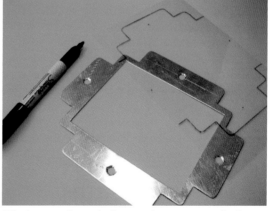

The butyrate is marked out and cut to size to fit the homemade frame.

the master so that the finished vac-form part is the same size as the master was before sanding. (If you have moulding materials then it is a good idea to take a casting of the work you have done so far because the heated-up butyrate may bond with your plastic master.)

It is important that the finished vac-form part has good register where you need to cut. There are several ways to help to achieve this. Make sure that the base of the master is at least half the height of the actual part.

Ensure that there is a definite 'step' where the base meets the master and that the base splays inwards and not outwards. Holes can be drilled at angles all the way around the step, and this too will help to suck the butyrate firmly over the lip of the master to give the needed register. Make sure that the drill holes go all the way through the base! Two further aspects determine good register – the strength of the vacuum cleaner and the molecular state of the butyrate just before it is plunged over the master. Make sure that the vacuum cleaner's cylinder is empty and that the toaster has been on twice before in immediate succession. And so with the vacuum cleaner on, and the toaster on its third run, hold the framed butyrate over the toaster (using pliers

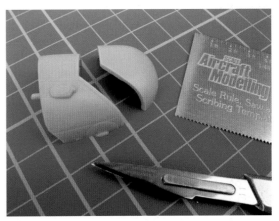

With the help of a razor saw like that produced by the magazine Scale Aircraft Modelling and a scalpel blade the solid plastic part to be remodelled into a clear part is removed.

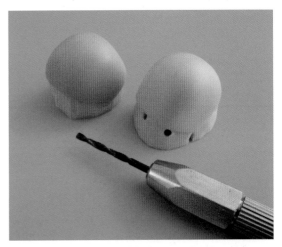

Some kits need more replacement transparencies than others. In the case of the Airfix 1/48 de Havilland Mosquito NF.30 all the clear parts need replacing, as well as the nose transforming from solid plastic to clear vac-form in order to model one of the decal options provided.

After any construction work that may be necessary is complete, the whole object is cut back 0.5mm in order for the vac-form copy to be the same dimensions as the original part. The object also needs to be mounted so that the butyrate has room to travel well past the master before starting to splay out or crease up. If you have the materials, making and then using a resin copy will be better due to the possibility of the heated butyrate bonding with the plastic original. A definite lip is required as well as suction holes to help the butyrate to give a well-defined edge to the clear part.

or some means of keeping your hands away from the heat source) until the sheet becomes floppy in the middle. When this happens, plunge the butyrate over the master sat on the grill, making sure that the frame makes firm contact with and compresses the draft excluder tape. The vacuum cleaner will do the rest. After about a minute turn off the vacuum cleaner and lift the frame. Due to the 'step' between the base and the master, the master will be firmly embedded into the butyrate and will only be released when you come to take a new scalpel to the well-registered lip of the part you have created. And that is DIY vac-form modelling!

The object is then sat securely on the grill over the chamber and with the cordless vacuum cleaner on the butyrate is held with pliers over the toaster to heat up.

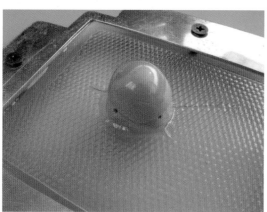

The flexible butyrate is then plunged on top of the object, making sure that the frame makes contact with the grill. If the butyrate has been heated up enough and the object has sufficient height you will have a perfect 0.5mm larger vac-form copy of your master object – in our case the Mosquito NF.30 nose.

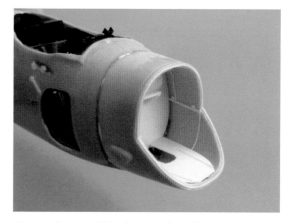

Due to the incredible thinness of vac-form parts it is preferable to increase the bonding area with the kit by attaching a small internal ledge for the vac-form to butt up against, giving the vac form items two planes on which to be glued using . . .

. . . PVA wood glue.

The results of your work are certainly very pleasing and rewarding. You may feel a little upset that the part wasn't provided in the kit, but you can console yourself with the knowledge that your vac-form part will be better than an injection-moulded kit part had it been available.

Vac-form parts will always be much thinner than the injection-moulded parts they are to replace. This gives ample width for a small lip to be cemented to the kit aperture just inboard of the outside line so that the clear vac-form part can butt up against it, being secured with PVA wood glue. The tiniest amounts of superglue can be run into the join line to give even greater strength, but any more than this amount risks having trapped cyanoacrylate vapour etch the surface of the clear part. This is known as 'fogging' or 'misting', and usually happens in oxygenated sealed areas when too much vapour has nowhere else to go.

It is not always necessary to fabricate a clear vac-form item from scratch. You may be able to get what you want by 'cross-kitting' two existing vac-form canopies, for example, to get the kind you want. Work starts with mounting the canopies onto some dental putty. This has the double advantage of both providing a solid core to cut into, as well as sufficiently dulling down the glare of the vac-form part so that you can see more clearly where to cut. Dymo tape, which can be found in most stationery shops, can then be cut into thinner lengths and applied around the area to be cut. Dymo tape is sufficiently deep to give a good guide to the new scalpel blade when cutting. This, plus the dulling effect of the dental putty, makes the task of cutting into vac-form canopies quite straightforward. The cross-kitted canopy can then have its constituent parts taped together ready for PVA wood glue to be run in. Once the inside has been detailed with decal strip, and whatever else you might wish, the canopy is ready to be fitted to the cockpit in much the same way as the clear nosepiece. Any poor join lines can be hidden by using decal strip (*see* Chapter 6).

PHOTO-NEGATIVE INSTRUMENT GAUGE DETAIL

Another aspect of clear part modelling involves the use of printed photo-negative instrument gauge detail. Such items come as counterparts to photo-etched brass control panels and are

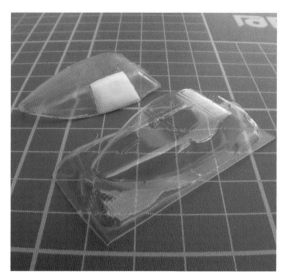

Canopies are a little harder to remodel. Fillers like Milliput can add the unique characteristics of the canopy, but cutting the whole canopy back 0.5mm is difficult. It is preferable to see if an excellent Falcon canopy is available, either sold in one of their sets or passed on as an individual item to Squadron/Signal to sell as part of their Crystal Clear range.

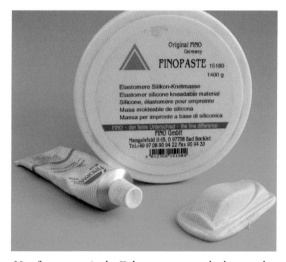

Vac-form canopies by Falcon are extremely shiny and a little flexible. Both these factors make them difficult to separate from their base. A matt pastel-coloured quick-curing putty like that used in the dental trade for taking impressions of teeth is very helpful, not only for providing a more solid structure to work with . . .

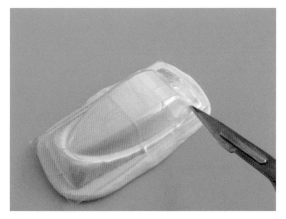

. . . but also dulling down the canopy glare enough so as to be able to see the join line better for cutting.

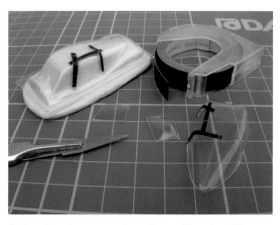

Using dental putty as a base, Dymo Tape (see Chapter 12) can also be used to guide the scalpel blade when altering two vac-form canopies.

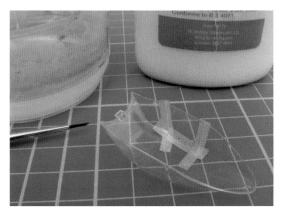

The altered vac-form canopy can then be put back together with PVA wood glue and small drops of Speed Epoxy for extra strength.

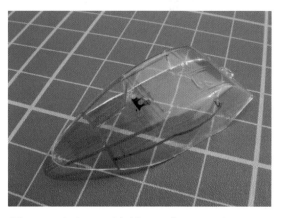

The extra clarity provided by vac-form canopies necessitates perhaps more internal detailing to the actual inside of the canopy than you would maybe want to do. With the Mosquito, however, you have little choice as the only real way to represent the internal framing is to apply strips of cockpit green decal to the inside of the vac-form canopy (see Chapter 6).

simple to use. The most important thing is to be able to appreciate the instrument detail after it has been sandwiched behind the photo-etched brass control panel. This means either painting the back of it the appropriate instrument gauge colour, or doing the same to the backing it is to be layered onto. The most important aspect is to make sure that the instrument detail lines up with the holes that have been punched out of the photo-etched brass control panel. When you are satisfied you have the correct register, run in some superglue at the join line in a number of places. With some acetate sheets/ photo-etched brass control panels it is not possible to go wrong. Layer the parts on top of each other and glue them with a slower drying material such as Humbrol Clearfix. The final step is to drop either more Clearfix or Clear

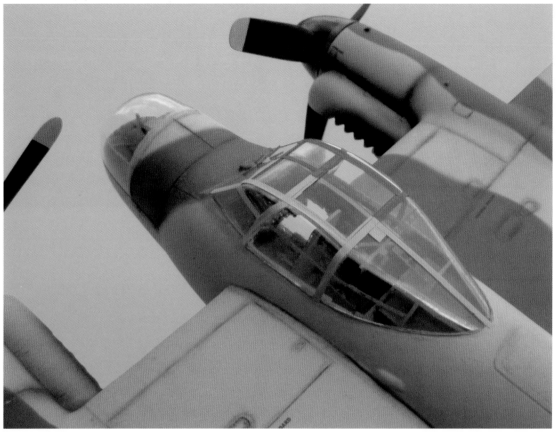

With the canopy in place on the cockpit, using the same principles as with the clear nose, decal strip can be used again to simulate the cockpit framing (see Chapter 6), which also is quite handy for masking any crude join lines.

Cote into the bezel apertures to give a glass-like finish.

These clear instrument items can, of course, be homemade using acetate purchased from a stationery shop. Paint one side of the acetate black. When this is dry, use the sharp point of a pin to scratch away the gauge detail and any writing on the face of the instrument. The scalpel blade can also be applied very usefully to get the finest of scratches (very handy for the face of a British-style compass). The hardest task is being able to scratch away detail in a true circle. If you have a hole punch set, then the appropriate punch can be selected and the black paint slightly indented. If not, you could paint the black on the acetate with the instrument panel overlaying it, thus getting only the areas painted black where there are corresponding instruments. Place the instrument panel face down onto the acetate after you have finished scratching the gauge detail. You will then have no need to cut out the individual gauges but only the shape of the whole instrument panel – turning the acetate non-paint-side-up the detail will correspond directly with the back of the instrument panel. At some stage prior to final assembly the painted side of the acetate should be over-painted in the lighter colours used for the instruments you are modelling. This shows through the scratched-off black to give very satisfying results. Any writing on the face of the instrument in a different colour can also be carefully picked out for a very professional multi-coloured instrument finish.

Clear Part Masks

Where the decision is made to spray paint on the canopy framing, precision masking is required. A quick and relatively inexpensive way of doing this is to use Eduard Express Mask set. These sets have one main drawback – the film used is too low-tack!

BELOW LEFT & RIGHT: The film is therefore unable to handle the slightest of compound curves and needs replacing with Tamiya masking tape or the like.

The film also has a short lifespan so that even the masks on flat surfaces start to peel off if you are performing the time-consuming 'artistic painting' technique as described in Chapter 5.

One of the great leaps forward in our hobby has been the development of photo-negative material on which is printed instrument dials. When either placed on a white background or painted white on the reverse side, only what you need to see is shown up. Most photo-etched brass sets and multimedia super-detail sets now come with this material.

With the photo-etched brass instrument panel lined up correctly and secured in place, drops of Humbrol Clear Cote can be dropped into the instrument bezels, both to create glass faces and to secure the instrument panel in place.

Much of this detail will be lost when the model is finished, but what can be seen is very impressive.

These impressive instrument details can be homemade by painting black onto one side of acetate, scratching off the details, covering the area over in the appropriate instrument gauge colours before turning over.

When punched or cut out these homemade instruments look great at zero cost and little effort.

NAVIGATION LIGHTS

One final area of modelling clear parts concerns navigation lights. These items attract attention and can make or break a model. Some kits do not come with clear injection-moulded parts for these areas; others do, but may unfortunately need replacing. Small blocks of perspex cut from a transparent toothbrush are an ideal solution for this most necessary work. Initial preparation involves the light interior being painted the appropriate colour, the reverse face of the perspex block polished up with various grades of polishing mesh (provided by SnJ amongst others), as well as holes being drilled into the

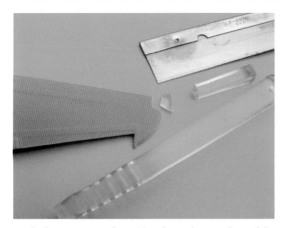

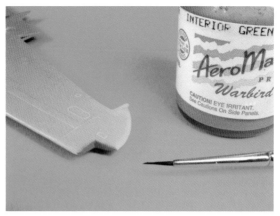

With the exception of 1/144 scale, perhaps scale models really need to have clear navigation lights when the type being modelled had clear Perspex-type covers. These are easily made if the kit either doesn't have them or in this case they have great big sinkholes in them. A chunk of clear perspex cut roughly to shape from a toothbrush will do the trick.

The faces of the kit's wing tip cutaways are pre-painted an appropriate interior colour.

reverse sides of the perspex blocks. These represent the bulbs; the holes then have the appropriate colour paint run into them. Making sure that the hole you have drilled is exactly in the middle of where you are going to fix the block, proceed to secure the blocks to the wings with superglue. Failure to get the bulb right in the middle risks the subterranean drill hole being exposed when the block is sanded down to shape. Drilling in only a very short distance will limit this threat significantly. Once secure, work can begin on sanding the block to shape, starting with a file or hobby drill attachments on low revolutions (being careful not to attack the plastic too much), and finishing with the polishing mesh mentioned earlier.

The finished result of clean, crisp and unique

Holes are then drilled centrally into the reverse faces of the perspex blocks and filled with either red or green paint. The semi-translucent colours by Humbrol are good for this.

clear parts on a model gives great satisfaction and is worth every minute spent on such a highly visible aspect of scale aircraft modelling.

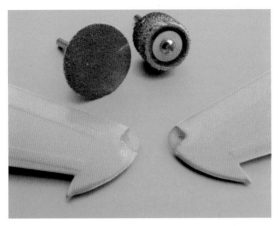

With the reverse faces of the perspex blocks firmly superglued in place the work of reshaping them can begin. A hobby drill and good transformer are helpful acquisitions.

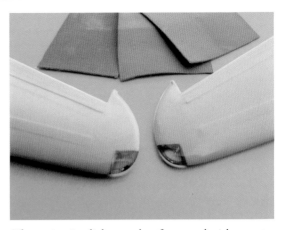

The navigation lights are then fine-tuned with various grades of wet and dry abrasive paper, culminating with the use of Micro Mesh cloths to polish up the perspex to a high sheen.

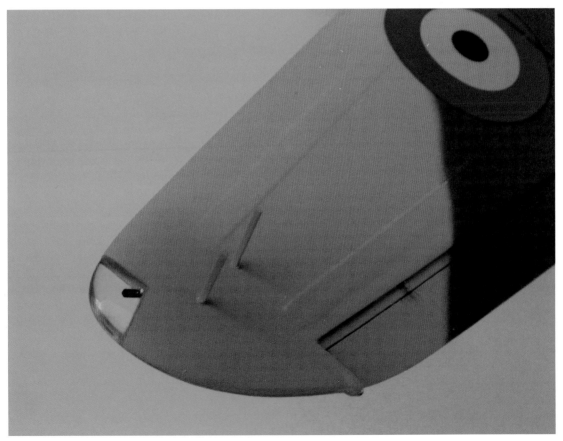

The finished result!

CHAPTER 5

Painting

The primary objective in painting scale model aircraft is 'effect'. Everything that is done has this one outcome in mind. In this chapter we note the two greatest ingredients that go into the mixing pot to achieve this coveted result – painting for scale and painting for effect.

SOLVING THE SCALE ISSUE

It is probably fair to say that the jury is still out on scale painting. Some argue that as the model is smaller than its real-life counterpart the pigments will be more compact, resulting in the overall model looking darker the smaller the scale. Others argue equally well that the aircraft should be painted lighter the smaller the scale, as the further away an object is the more diffused its vibrancy. Four things at least seem certain. Firstly, we view things subjectively; the human eye can perceive an incredible 3,000 variations in colour, and colour perception varies among people. Secondly, as stated elsewhere there is something most unrealistic about being able to view a scale model. Thirdly, different colours and shapes react differently to the changing strength and direction of sunlight, which is in turn affected by distance. Fourthly, paint supplies for real aircraft will vary depending on the batch and the manufacturer's interpretation of the colour, coupled with wear and tear. It is not surprising that a colour photo of a line-up of Blackburn Buccaneers showed twenty-five different shades of Ocean Grey! As can be appreciated, it is difficult to come to any solid conclusions when such a vast array of factors has a bearing on what it

means to finish your subject in a scale-friendly manner.

Are there any rules we can follow at all? 'Don't worry about it' is not the answer – you might get it wrong, but you do not want to if you can help it is the attitude this book is trying to encourage. In a way, the issue of scale painting only comes into sharp focus when painting model aircraft at the extreme ends of the scales, for example 1/144 and 1/24. The only other time that scale will become an issue is when you have two aircraft in the same livery but two different scales parked next to each other on the shelf. Having such models painted in the same colours but with no appreciable contrast just looks wrong and is to be avoided. One way of avoiding the problem of 'scale painting' is simply to build models in one scale only! At first this might seem to be something of a cop-out, but given the amazing variables involved there is nothing to say that the paint taken straight from the tin or jar won't be just the right colour for the scale you prefer to model in – even here there will be variables depending on the batch of paint, what medium you use to dilute the paint for spraying, how much you dilute it, what pressure you spray it at and doubtless other variables besides. Unfortunately such an option is only half a solution and very limiting indeed.

When more than one scale is modelled, relying on the variables from paint taken straight from the tin or jar alone will not be enough and other measures need to be taken. No collective decision has been reached regarding the best

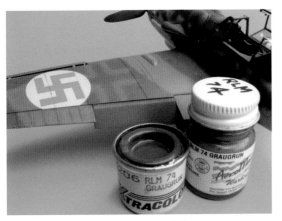

The same colour can have as many different interpretations as suppliers! Here the Luftwaffe RLM 74 Graugrün (Grey/Green) by Xtracolor and that by AeroMaster can be seen used together. The AeroMaster paint (now produced under the PolyScale label) is much lighter and has been used to simulate a Finnish 'homebrew' to cover the German national markings on the wings of this Bf 109G-6. Such differences in interpretations of colour can help in the quest to paint model aircraft in a scale-friendly manner.

approach, so it will be up to you to form your own conclusions by trial and error. If, for example, after experimenting you think that smaller scale model aircraft look better lighter and larger scales darker stick to that and vice versa. Sometimes the work will have been done for you as two manufacturers may produce paints labelled as the same colour, but those produced by one manufacturer may be consistently darker, or lighter, than those same paints produced by the other manufacturer. If this is the case, a simple enough guide is to use consistently one make for one scale and the alternative make for the other scale. It will be noted that in Chapter 8 that the 1/72 Tamiya Spitfire Mk V (converted into a Mk II) has been sprayed in the lighter PolyScale rendering of British Dark Green, whereas the Airfix 1/48 de Havilland Mosquito, which appears in various places in this book, has been sprayed with the darker rendering of the same colour paint produced by Xtracolor. The difference is enough to suggest scale.

Masking Off

It is not just the paint you use that can help to suggest the scale of the model, but how you mask off ready for spraying as well. An understanding of the original object is of utmost importance in determining the best way to apply scale painting. Two very common examples would be the RAF's use of freehand 'feathered edge' disruptive pattern and the Luftwaffe's WWII 'splinter pattern' disruptive scheme. This latter scheme was also done freehand but much tighter, sprayed tightly to a pre-masked border. In the world of modelling this equates to an extremely hard-edged pattern in 1/72 scale. You just do not see trace amounts of overspray 72ft away from the real aircraft. Of course, it is a relatively simple matter to mask off hard edges using liquid and fabric masking products, but whilst achieving the correct look they can also create problems as it is very hard to prevent paint building up along the line of the masking join, even if using fewer coats. The resulting raised edge to the camouflage pattern can be seen the clearest whilst the model is in a glossed state ready for decals, and although much of the unwanted ridges seem to disappear under a few coats of matt varnish, decals that are extra thin will be an unfortunate reminder to you of this problem as any ridges will show up through them.

The three scales looked at in this chapter, 1/72, 1/48 and 1/32. Not only do the paints change but how you mask off camouflage also. In 1/72 scale hard-edge masking is in order, in 1/48 a feathered edge with Blu-Tack and in 1/32 a freehand application can be attempted.

Fabric masks like Tamiya hobby tape are a good but wasteful way of masking out areas for a 1/72 hard-edge pattern prior to another application of paint. Here the Ju 88H-1 profiled in Chapter 9 has had its typical Luftwaffe splinter pattern masked in preparation for the darker RLM 70 Schwartzgrun (Black-Green) paint. Although the tape doesn't have that strong a tack it is advisable to peel it off slowly to avoid tearing up paint back to the primer, or even paint and primer back to the plastic or resin.

Masking fluids like that produced by Humbrol are the lazy man's alternative to the fabric style of masks and can be used to simulate hard-edge masking in 1/72. It is best used on top of gloss surfaces as it can, if used thinly, have a tendency to try to bond with very matt surfaces. It is also difficult to rip out of hinge lines and the like. Paint sprayed onto the cured fluid will shatter and flake everywhere when being peeled off so can be messy. When being used to mask canopies and other clear parts it is best to remove the masking fluid after each stage of priming and painting, as too many layers on top of the masking fluid make it increasingly more difficult to remove.

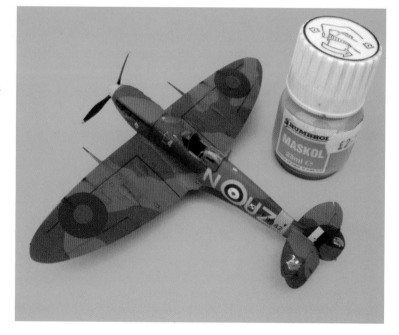

Extreme care needs to be taken to try to decrease any build-up where decals are going to be placed, although this is easier said than done. The finest of Micromesh polishing cloths can be used with plenty of water, but care needs to be taken not to upset the surrounding paint too much. The best answers are either to try to avoid repeated passes over the model at the tapes edge, or to spray with a number of fine strokes just inside the border, working away from the border all the time so as to keep the build-up of paint over the tape edge to a minimum. While the finish can look a bit streaky, it does cut down considerably on the unwanted build-up. One final preventative measure is to remove the masking by peeling it off with a motion adjacent to the fresh camouflage, lessening the danger of pulling the paint up. Indeed, if the model has been left to dry long enough this should not happen, but it is better to be safe than sorry. Of course, the most ideal use of hard-edged masking is when the masking follows the kit's panel lines. This applies to all scales, but is really only limited to bare metal finishes (see the box pp.67–68 on metal finishes).

The larger the scale, the more obvious the freehand application of paint on the original can be. In 1/48 scale one acceptable way of

Micromesh cloth in various grits.

depicting this is with the help of materials such as Blu-Tack. This material is rolled into thin sausages and tacked onto the aircraft in such a way as to achieve the correct disruptive pattern. The environs of patterns not to be painted are then masked out ready for spraying. One essential prerequisite for this material to give a perfectly tight but noticeable feathered edge in 1/48 scale is consistency. The airbrush needs to pass over the same spot at the same angle every time to avoid a multitude of different feathered edges. This is more easily achieved on the wings and horizontal tail planes where direct overhead passes can be made, but more difficult on the fuselage where the compound curve of the structure necessitates change in direction. Nevertheless it can be done, and done well, without any of the difficulties arising from hard-edge masking. Occasionally the Blu-Tack will leave a slight residue where it has been tacked onto the surface of the primary colour, especially where the primary colour has a matt finish. This will come off with a bit of water, but is less likely to happen when the Blu-Tack has been applied to a gloss paint finish.

With a good airbrush the same effect gained by using Blu-Tack to apply the upper camouflage colours on a 1/48 subject can be achieved freehand in 1/32. Masking can also be minimized by painting the model in stages; for instance, spraying the fuselage first, followed, when dry, by the horizontal surfaces of the

The difficulty of hard-edge masking – paint build up at the conflux of colours causing ridges. This can be kept to a minimum by either more careful spraying or rubbing down with micromesh cloths.

main and tail planes. The freehand technique is not in any way time-saving, but is good experience all the same. The best way to achieve freehand camouflage application is to set the airbrush to spray a slightly thinner than normal paint mix with a very small needle aperture and to spray at between 8 and 12psi. The above set-up is used carefully to mark out the borders of the camouflage pattern and then, keeping the same set-up, to block in the appropriate area with the appropriate colour. The procedure is

Blu-Tack rolled into thin sausages is a great way, in conjunction with other masking materials, to get a nice feathered edge in 1/48. Here the Airfix 1/48 de Havilland NF.30 profiled elsewhere in the book is getting the treatment . . .

. . . the final result. When sprayed over at a consistent angle, the Blu-Tack does a really nice job.

then repeated with the next camouflage colour, but with even more care.

Air Brushing

Whereas an amount of controversy exists regarding scale painting, one area of advanced scale aircraft modelling that is not in any question is the need for a good airbrush and compressor to accomplish both scale painting and painting for effect. Your budget will probably be the most determining factor in what you purchase, and much of this topic has already been covered in Mark Stanton's book on *Scale Aircraft Modelling*; but just let me recap by saying that you will not regret purchasing a twin, or duel, action airbrush of good reputation, as well as a compressor with a water-trap and the ability to regulate the pressure setting. Airbrushing is all about control, so it stands to reason that the more set-up

There are times when, with confidence, you can get away without masking at all. Freehand spraying is usually restricted to the larger scales, but not always, and my 1/72 Academy F-15E Strike Eagle back dated to an Israeli D looked like a possibility. It will be noted that the Air Supremacy paint schemes of the F-15As and Ds can be seen to 'bleach' into one another when faded and as there was not much contrast in the PolyScale acrylic Dark and Light Ghost Grey a freehand application of the Dark Ghost Grey was possible with the help of a little pressure and a watery mix.

options your airbrush and compressor can give you, the more control you will have.

Owning the right equipment naturally leads to the important question of where to use it. Even with some sort of extractor fan set up spraying is an unsociable activity due to the smell, mess and other potential hazards, so if your actions affect others, others will probably have a say in where you spray! Not everyone has the luxury of spraying in the most ideal place, if such a place exists, or even spraying where they would like to, but three factors need to be paramount in setting up: light, oxygen and as sterile an environment as possible. Without light you cannot see what you are doing, so all the money spent on equipment to give you as much control as possible is wasted. If you are able to spray at times and in a location with ample natural or 'Tongan Light' then great, but this is probably too idealistic a possibility for most. Again, it costs money, but for spray bays set up in more dingy corners there are some excellent hobby lamps available, such as the ones produced by the Daylight Company. A fresh air supply is a vital health precaution; bad vapours and dust particles can be kept out of the lungs by using a good mask and evacuated

out of the room by an extractor fan. Finally, one of the greatest headaches whilst spraying is the presence of dust and fibre particles that settle on the model and become embedded in the wet paint. Achieving a sterile environment is not possible, but we have all seen how much rubbish is floating around in the air when the sun shines into the living room. Every time we move or touch material objects clouds of semi-invisible fibres are launched into orbit. Spraying in an area devoid of material, like a garage, naturally cuts down on such unwanted foreign objects in our wet paint, but even here one has to contend with dust being stirred up from the floor and being blown in from outside through the garage door. Even the extractor fan, which is designed to help, will hinder by attracting air infested with unwanted fibres into the very area in which you are spraying!

There is really no complete escape from dust and fibres; we just have to co-habit with them. If you have to spray in a material-rich room, hoover and dust well beforehand, wait a good while for things to settle, then move slowly to your spray bay and begin, covering the model as soon as possible afterwards. Using acrylic paints obviously has an advantage here in that

A good twin action airbrush and compressor with water trap and pressure regulator are to be preferred over single action airbrushes and standard compressors when it comes to painting for effect. Iwata Equipment available via The Airbrush Company is among the best you could wish to work with.

My little den in the garage. Note the use of an old cooker hob extractor fan.

the paint dries far quicker and thus the model is exposed to the danger of embedded fibres for a shorter time. If modelling in a garage, mop the concrete floor, wipe down the immediate spraying area with a damp cloth and proceed to spray whilst everything around you is still wet. This

not only 'beds down' any remaining floor dust but helps to raise the humidity levels, which in turn lower the static levels. Again, cover the model as soon as possible after spraying.

It is always good housekeeping to wash your injection-moulded kit or resin aftermarket set

By far the most obvious candidate for freehand spraying will be 1/32. This was a very popular scale when I was a boy thanks to the Matchbox kits. It is still a popular scale and the Hasegawa kits like this 1/32 Messerschmitt Bf 109G-6 are fantastic value for money as well as presenting perfect targets to practise scale freehand spraying. (Thanks to Model Design Construction Ltd for supplying the Finnish decal options.)

Freehand painting is best completed in stages, for instance spraying the camouflage on the fuselage first, the idea being that you have the wings to hold onto for maximum stability whilst carefully spraying at close quarters.

When the fuselage is dry the horizontal surfaces can be tackled with very little masking to the fuselage needed at all.

with soapy water or mineral spirits. This removes any trace elements of chemicals inherent in the manufacturing process. A lint-free cloth and soft old toothbrush are ideal for this work. It might seem like a waste of energy, but for the nine times you would have got away with it there will be one time when you won't!

Pre-washing your model to remove any chemicals from the manufacturing process might not prove to be necessary but is good housekeeping.

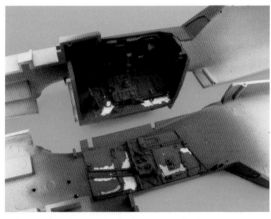

This is what happens when you get caught out! Traces of chemicals on the Model Design Construction Limited Bf 109G-6 resin cockpit detail set prevented the primer and paint adhering to the surface of the resin – consequently it blistered up and then flaked off.

PAINTING FOR EFFECT

We now come to the second main point in our subject – that of painting for effect. This kind of painting takes much longer due to the multiple applications needed to produce highlights and lowlights. It is also a little more expensive in terms of the increased use of airbrush cleaner between the multiple stages, but it all begins like any other style of spray painting – by making sure that the object or area you are to spray is ready, being free from foreign bodies and chemical traces before priming. Aerosol automotive primers as well as those used in the fantasy Warhammer hobby are excellent materials for priming, creating a very tough surface area that will not easily scratch off back to the bare plastic or other material. Caution is needed with these paints, however, due to the fumes and the large quantities of spray dust created by such a wide arc of paint delivery, as well as the very real danger of paint build-up. These kinds of paints have a semi-filling capability and fine-scale panel detail can easily be lost by applying too many coats or by spraying too close to the model. Equally dangerous is spraying too far away from the model in an attempt to create a thinner coat. It

The next step in the artistic painting of a dark coloured cockpit like our Hasegawa Bf 109G-6 – the application of the base colour, in this case RLM 66 Schwartzgrau (Dark/Black Grey).

is much more likely that you will achieve a very 'rough' coat, as you will have laid on more spray dust than spray paint! Practising on a scrap model aeroplane is the best way to get to grips with this helpful but demanding medium.

Next comes the application, which can be an immensely rewarding and enjoyable procedure. The process begins by pre-shading the model's panel and working part detail with a tight pattern of mucky black/brown paint. The spraying has to be kept as tight as possible to the detail to achieve the desired results. This is especially challenging the smaller the scale. Spraying indiscriminately just will not work. Different consistencies of paint mix at different air pressures and needle apertures will give you a good understanding of what your airbrush can achieve and what looks the best. If you have never used this procedure before it is probably best, as with most spraying techniques, to start off on a larger scale model to gain experience and confidence. There are variations on a theme, of course, and one would not bother to pre-shade with a mucky black/brown spray mixture panel lines that would afterwards be covered in too dark a paint to allow the previous work to show up – the whole purpose would be lost. In this case, the dark base colour is applied first and instead has two applications of 'post-shading',

one dark, the other light, rather than a pre- and post-application of the lowlight and highlight method. If, however, the primary paint colour were of a lighter shade then pre-shading the panel lines first would normally be the first step.

Where the area being sprayed is rather busy – like a cockpit – even more depth can be added to the sprayed lowlights by running pure black thinned-out oil paint into the detail. With a final paint mix just a fraction lighter than the uniform base coat the area is 'dusted' to pick up the raised detail so that we now have highlights as well as lowlights. Once any areas that would receive greater wear have been dry brushed with even lighter shades of the primary colour or colours (using a soft-cropped chisel brush), any detail work and weathering is painted or applied to conclude the painting for effect process in the cockpit.

As for exterior artistic painting, the pre-painted lowlights are often enough to accentuate the panel detail, leaving any use of run-in oil paints restricted to inspection hatches and moving parts. Another aspect of artistic painting that differs from that applied to a cockpit is the fact that exterior painting will normally be multi-coloured. The aim is not to obliterate totally the pre-painted lowlights; both over-

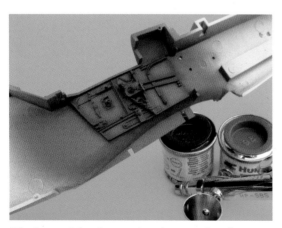

The Iwata airbrush comes into its own when the next step requires a mucky black/brown mix sprayed discriminately over the detail of the cockpit.

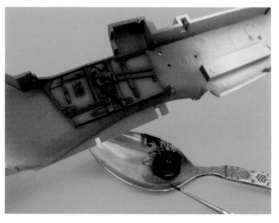

This is further backed up by running diluted artist's black oil paint into the detail, allowing capillary action to do most of the work.

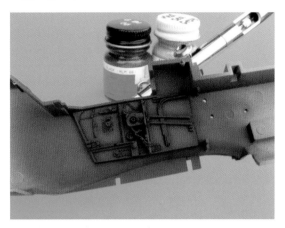

With the lowlight work completed in the cockpit the whole cockpit can then be 'dusted' with a slightly lighter shade of the base colour. Spraying across the detail rather than face on to it will limit the highlights to the raised surfaces.

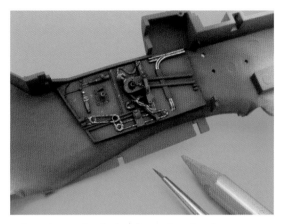

The cockpit is finished with any fine detail painting, paint chipping and extra dry brushing to contact areas as required.

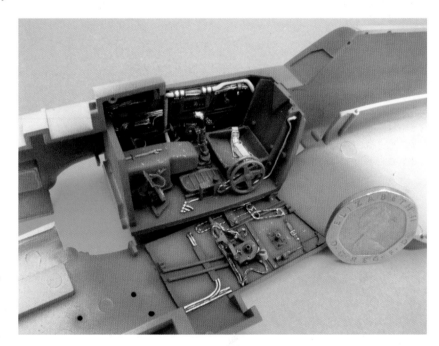

The reward of what is a much slower but enjoyable way of painting your model.

lapping colours and darker shades of camouflage will tend to do this, necessitating the reapplication of the lowlights followed by the colours that obliterated them. Here is a strong argument for either being more careful or for a procedure for exterior painting similar to cockpit painting whereby all the primary colours are applied before any lowlights are sprayed. The lowlights are then, with perhaps even greater care and precision, applied to the panel detail on top of the base colours and then lightly sprayed over with the appropriate base colours until the desired effect is achieved. However you prefer to accomplish the lowlight stage, the next stage of exterior painting needs great discernment in order to establish where to apply a slightly lighter mix of the primary colour to create the highlights. It is important not to overdo this step – limiting your highlights to a few bumps and ridges will be far better than 'dusting' the whole area as you would the cockpit.

Painting for effect can be applied to every part that makes up a kit, turning flat-looking kit parts into three-dimensional objects and three-dimensional kit parts into parts that look like they would really work. It is not a process for those looking for a quick build nor does it lend itself well to smaller scales, but its use will revolutionize the look of your models.

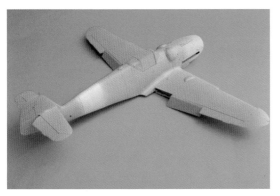

Painting the exterior of an aircraft begins the same way as with the cockpit, by priming it.

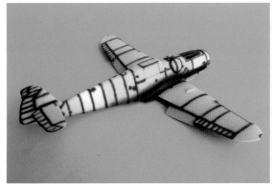

Using very little pressure and a watery mix of black or black/brown, the Iwata airbrush and compressor come into their own again as all the exterior panel lines and other details are pre-shaded.

Work then begins on applying the colours particular to your subject, the idea being to almost but not quite obliterate the pre-shading.

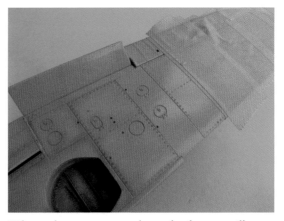

Where colours meet or overlap each other you will inevitably be layering too many coats of paint on top of the pre-shading. The panel lines in these areas will simply need to be gone over again followed by a fresh coat of the colour responsible for obliterating them.

The same situation occurs when the camouflage colours are too dark and although the pre-shading is still visible it would benefit from being reapplied.

The results of applying the painting-for-effect techniques to the exterior surfaces of your model are stunning, the pre-shading being quite noticeable on lighter colours such as the RLM 76 Lichtblau (Blue Grey) and RLM 04 Gelb (Yellow) on our BF 109G-6 . . .

. . . and on the white segment of the BF 109G-6 spinner.

The results of the pre-shading of the darker upper camouflage colours of RLM 74 Graugrün (Grey Green) and RLM 75 Grauviolett (Grey Violet) are far more subtle, hardly being done justice by the camera, but they look great all the same.

At various stages of the painting process lighter shades of the primary colours are used sparingly to highlight detail, be it a pinch of white in the yellow to pick out the spine of the Eastern Front theatre band, or . . .

. . . in the Grauviolett to pick out the wheel clearance bulges on the upper wings, or in the Graugrün to pick out the bulges forward of the windscreen to clear the breaches of the MG 13 weapons.

Metal Finishes

For many years modellers have either shied away from natural metal finishes altogether, contenting themselves with modelling 'doped aluminium' clad aircraft or have persevered with the demanding technique of overlaying the model with tin foil, or the extremely messy system of SnJ spray and powder.

Thankfully a company called Alclad II came along and offered a more sensible alternative to foil and buffing powders. Now with a very wide range of metallic finishes most projects can be planned accordingly without beads of sweat forming on the brow. Here Andrew Eaton displays his 1/72 Academy F-86 Sabre sprayed with a number of different shades of Alclad II, some straight from the jar, others mixed with each other. The product has no need to be thinned down and is best sprayed at about 20psi onto as smooth a primed surface as possible. The amazingly quick drying time of these Alclad II paints means that after just fifteen minutes of the most dominant metallic shade being sprayed on, hard Tamiya masking tape can be applied to the surrounds of various panels before they are over sprayed in a different metallic finish.

Automotive aerosol canned paints like Nissan Silver by Halfords can be used to give a simple but effective doped aluminium finish like that applied to this Tasman re-release of the Heller 1/72 Dragon Rapide in the markings of a Royal New Zealand Air Force de Havilland Dominie.

Another metal paint in the Alclad II range is Jet Exhaust, which is great for any exhaust stubs on propeller aircraft as well as the more obvious jet engine nozzles.

The Alclad II Chrome paint has a different formula; whereas the other Alclad II paints can be mixed with each other, the Alclad II Chrome cannot. Another difference is that the other Alclad II paints cannot be sprayed onto enamel surfaces whereas Alclad II Chrome has to be sprayed onto a pre-sprayed gloss black enamel surface in order to look the way it does – which is quite fantastic!

The oleo leg of the 1/32 Hasegawa Bf 109G-6 before being masked off until the very end of the project.

The Chrome finish of the 1/32 Hasegawa Bf 109G-6 is admittedly rather concealed and not done any justice to by the photograph but what can be seen is great. Thank you, Alclad II, for a wonderful product!

Metal 'stressed' skin aircraft are invariably covered with light aluminium and aluminium (Duralumin) alloy materials, the exception being where more heat-resistant metals are required; thus many gun covers and the leading edges of fast jet wings are made from steels and jet engine covers made from titanium. As with everything else in this book good reference photographs are the key to understanding the subject in hand.

CHAPTER 6

Decaling

For many modellers this is the really exciting part where the model aircraft starts to take on its own unique character, a point not lost on those companies producing hundreds of decal sheets to cater for every whim and fancy. Some 32,000 Bf 109 Messerschmitts were produced during WWII – I think at least 22,000 of them must be covered by decal options by now, or at least that's how it seems! Sometimes, however, due to missing, damaged or unavailable decals it will be necessary to make your own markings using either stencils, or white and clear blank decal paper for ink-jet printers.

Both fabric and photo-etched brass templates exist for a number of air forces' national insignia. Less complicated stencils, such as that needed for the Japanese Hinomora, for exam-ple, can be created quite simply using Frisk Film. The advantage of using Frisk Film lies in it being transparent, which aids positioning, but it is also low tack enough to reposition until set correctly. However, there are also a number of pitfalls, as the material is very difficult to cut through, with an Olfa circular cutter needing to be at the extreme limit of its circumference. A much cleaner cut is achieved by drawing the circle and then cutting it out by hand carefully with a scalpel. The low-tack aspect, whilst helping in some ways, hinders in others, as a certain amount of bleeding or 'creep under' can occur during paint spraying. This is due in the most part to having to use the Olfa cutter at such an extreme angle that it causes the Frisk Film to tear rather than cut.

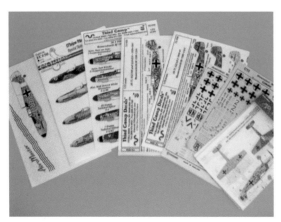

One way of achieving a unique aircraft model – aftermarket decals. The options are almost endless!

The traditional way of going about water-slide decaling – a good gloss surface and the excellent setting solutions produced by Microscale.

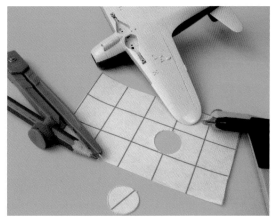

Basic templates can be cut out from materials such as Frisk Film.

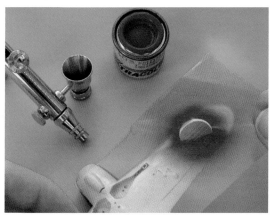

The design is positioned and then sprayed over. The benefit of using Frisk Film is that it is clear so that you can see exactly where you are positioning the template on the model.

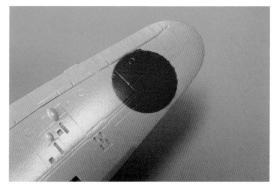

The downside of Frisk Film is that it is quite low tack so 'creep under' can occur and will need tidying up.

Blank (water slide) decal paper is a marvellous material to have stored away in your inventory. It comes in either a clear or a white format, and can even be purchased with ink-jet printers in mind. Offcuts of decal paper can be sprayed with either acrylic or enamel paints to provide you with your own 'decal palette' from which to select and then cut out basic markings. When sprayed with an aircraft interior colour first, followed by the upper camouflage livery, decal paper becomes a very handy way to produce excellently thin canopy framing, negating the need for time-consuming masking. For this purpose, it is best to cut the appropriate widths of decal paper from the unpainted, reverse side. This prevents any cracking or indenting of the paint caused by the scalpel blade digging into it. In Chapter 4, mention is made of dental putty being used to fill out the cavity of vac-form canopies. The resulting impression comes in handy in more ways than mentioned above, for you now have a means of gauging the various lengths of decal strip needed for the canopy framing. The decal strip is held in place and manipulated over the various contours of the canopy mould, following the canopy framing detail. The ability to slice through the decal strip, into the putty, at the point where the detail ends saves the considerable trouble of having to remove poorly measured wet decal strip from the model for alterations.

REPLICATING DAMAGED DECALS

Perhaps the most adventurous use of blank decal paper is with a personal computer, scanner and ink-jet printer. With this set-up, damaged decals can be replicated. One unfortunate reality of modelling older kits is that the varnishes used on the decal options in earlier days were not as good as they are today and are likely to have 'yellowed'. This effectively rules out their use, as the yellowing covers the markings as well as the carrier film. So what can be done? Many computers come with additional software for manipulating digital

Another way of decaling your model is to use some of the many good clear or white-backed decal sheets that are available.

Colours can also be sprayed in layers for cockpit framing. The interior colour is painted first, followed by the exterior camouflage colour.

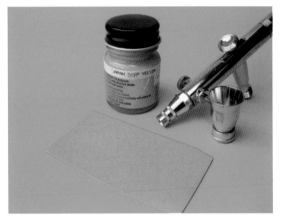

Decal sheet can be used to spray large blocks of colour onto . . .

The desired width of cockpit framing is then cut from the reverse side of the decal paper to avoid indenting the paint on the other side.

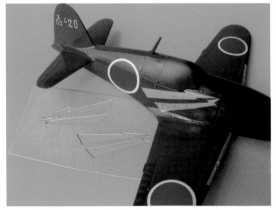

. . . which in turn can be used to cut out designs for normal decal application.

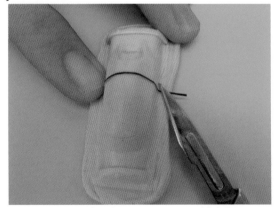

Dental putty has another use here as the impressions taken to help cut out vac-form canopies can also be used to measure more accurately just how much decal strip you will need at any one time.

71

The decal strip is then applied over the canopy frame detail just like any other decal, but with care to get it the right side up.

The results of both making your own markings, providing markings not supplied in the kit (like the red 'no walking' demarcation lines seen on this Hasegawa 1/72 Raiden 'Jack' and making sure that the canopy has nice, crisp detail, are most rewarding.

photography with links to a scanner; these photographic suites are an essential ingredient in this work. The yellowed decal sheet is placed onto the scanner bed and scanned in at high resolution, at least 600dpi (dots per inch). For the sake of simplicity we will say that the decal sheet has just two kinds of markings on it – solid black markings and solid white markings. The scan as 'black and white document' facility of the scanner effectively removes all colour, leaving only pure black markings on a pure white background. The resulting work can then be copied in the photo suite and pasted into a Microsoft Word document. Once the layout of the object has been set to 'square' it can be moved freely around the Word document page to wherever you want it to be for printing. Be careful not to resize the object in the process. It is then a simple case of loading the printer with the clear decal paper and selecting the 'print' icon. The finished product is a perfect copy of your black markings devoid of any yellow whatsoever!

White markings follow a similar procedure but need a little more work. Traditionally, the only real way to print white markings is by either owning or having access to an ALPS printer, like the ALPS MD-5000 colour printer, which has up to 2400dpi resolution. ALPS printers are the only printers that can print white; they also print in passes, so by

Another way of using these clear and white decal sheets is not to spray onto them, but to print on them with an ink-jet printer. Designs such as these 93rd Bombardment Wing markings can (with the publisher's permission) be scanned into the computer and played around with before being printed onto the white-backed decal paper. The same procedure can be used for hand-drawn designs like this small Luftwaffe badge of 3.(F)/123 reconnaissance unit seen on the right of the photograph that was needed for the Ju 88H-1 project seen in Chapter 9.

White and clear decal paper for ink-jet printers can be used to replace older decal sheets where the older style of varnish used has yellowed over time.

instructing the printer not to eject the paper after each pass, multi-colour designs can be printed with very good registration. These still come up from time to time on Internet auctions, but as the ink cartridges needed have been discontinued we will not be looking at this method. As before, scan in the yellowed decal sheet at 600dpi at least, but this time as an 'illustration'. The resulting picture in your photographic suite is thus in colour, showing all the yellowing. Unfortunately, the contrast between the once pure white markings and the overriding yellowing is too small for the 'flood fill' option in 'alter image' to be able to distinguish between marking and backing. This can be somewhat improved upon back at the scanner by altering the gamma and brightness levels of the scanned-in decal so that the yellow becomes light grey. The alteration is not foolproof, but the 'flood fill' option will find it

Andrew Eaton's wonderful B-52G with homemade 93rd Bombardment Wing decals printed on white decal paper and applied to a white background for extra obacity.

far easier to distinguish between a light grey background and off-white markings than between the previous off-yellow and off-white.

But how can this be used as a decal? In order to use white markings you need to use the white printable decal paper, but for the markings to be distinguishable you need also to print at the same time the colour of the background they will be applied to. This is a little tricky if the markings are going onto a camouflaged background, but where solid colours are concerned the best you can hope to do is to flood-fill the background of your scanned-in decals the appropriate colour. With the white markings flood-filled pure white and the backing sheet flood-filled the desired colour it is then necessary, under magnification, to tidy up the borders of the white markings as best you can with the paintbrush tool, set at various 'custom' levels for careful pixel work, as the 'flood fill' option has limits. The finished remedial work is then, as before, copied into a Word document and placed where you want it to appear on the decal paper. This time, the 'white' decal paper is loaded into the printer for a perfect reproduction of the white markings you thought were lost forever. Of course, there are some drawbacks and limitations to this method, but as long as the backing colour matches as closely

as possible the aircraft's paint scheme, when it comes to cutting out closely the individual white decal markings and placing them on the aircraft any traces of coloured decal backing should hopefully blend right in with a little help from a paintbrush.

It is highly unlikely that you will have so

Another way of making your own markings is to take photographs of the real aircraft you want to model. Here the Brooklands' badge of David Elliot's de Havilland DH60M Gypsy Moth is photographed. Thankfully, all the fuselage markings were on virtually flat surfaces, which made the process of converting the photographs into decals much easier.

The next step is to go into 'alter image' in your photographic suite and 'flood fill' the background with solid black (in this case) to eliminate flash-reflection and the like. The paintbrush tool will be of use to tidy up what 'flood fill' misses.

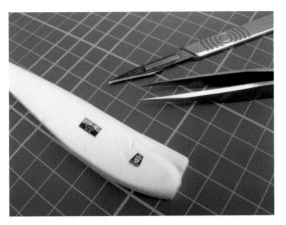

The design is then copied over to a Microsoft Word document, positioned and then printed onto normal paper. This allows you to make inexpensive test copies of the markings in order to get the right size.

many projects on the go that you will need all the space on the rather expensive clear or white decal sheet. You need either to wait till it is all filled up or go ahead with your project by having the objects printed in the middle of the paper, thus enabling the sheet to run through the printer at a later date without jamming. Simply save the Word document as a template and add future projects around the one in the centre to avoid printing designs where no decal paper exists anymore. When it comes to printing all you have to do is to delete the original markings in the centre before carrying on. The printed image will almost certainly subsequently need to be sealed in. Hand-painting on varnish or Johnson's Clear floor polish is highly risky as it can disturb the ink, even after a considerable time. Spraying on very thin coats of a custom-designed product, like that manufactured under the Microscale product range, or acrylic varnish from your airbrush is the best answer, but even here there is a risk of bleeding if too much wet varnish settles in one place. Sealing markings in can be done whilst the printed designs are still part of the otherwise empty decal sheet, but consider that all you are doing is spraying over blank areas where future projects will go. By the time you come to your last project the printed designs might be on a

backing sheet twice the thickness as it was originally! Sealing the present project in after the individual markings have been carefully cut from the decal sheet is the best answer.

Be very careful how you handle ink-jet printed designs. Even after they have been sealed in they can give you problems. It is best not to make contact with the printed area at all. It is also best to get the design off the wet backing sheet as quickly as possible, so obviously you only want to be working on one marking at a time. Laying the design face down after it has been dipped in water has the benefit of being able to push away the backing sheet from the decal rather than pushing the face-up decal away from the backing sheet, thus limiting contact

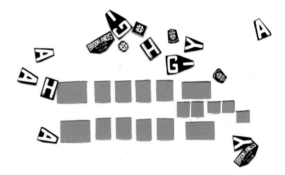

The printed designs are cut from the centre of the otherwise empty decal sheet to avoid the paper jamming in the printer at a later date.

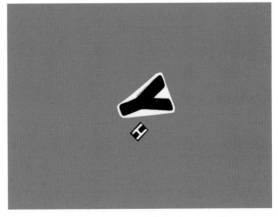

Even with the thinnest coats of acrylic varnish it is possible to cause the ink to bleed.

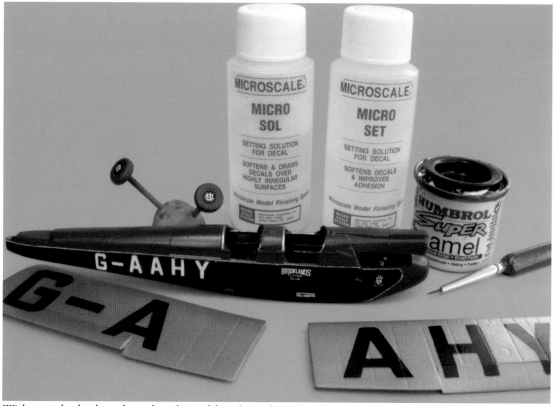

With care, the decals are located on the model in the traditional manner using Microscale Set and Sol on a gloss background. The previous work of printing out copies of the markings on normal paper has paid dividends.

The finished result – a truly unique model thanks to white and clear decal paper designed for ink-jet printers.

with the printable area. A paintbrush can then be used to turn over the decal gently and place it on the model.

Not only can these white and clear decal papers be used with a personal computer and scanner to replicate damaged decals, but they can also be used to produce your own decals. This is a great way to get a truly unique aircraft model and can be achieved in four ways:

1. The modeller needs to be good at drawing.
2. Permission can be sought and gained from a publisher to scan in images from one of their books. (It is illegal under the current European and International Copyright Laws to copy anything without the prior per-mission of the artist/author, plus it is illegal regardless of the above to distribute copies of anything without permission for such distribution, even if it is done without charge.)
3. The modeller can take photographs of the markings on the real aircraft for manipu-lating on the computer.
4. The modeller can use computer art packages such as Microsoft Paint, Corel Draw, AutoCAD and Adobe Illustrator. Whatever the case, it is simply a matter of using clear ink-jet decal paper for black markings and white ink-jet decal paper for white and colour markings. Where the marking is made up of white and colour but with a black border, white paper must still be used, but obviously with much greater care in cutting out the decal to remove any trace of white backing.

Scanning in photographs of someone else's artwork (with permission) for conversion into a decal marking needs a very high resolution to capture as much detail as possible. These images can generate quite large file sizes, but this does mean that when it comes to shrinking the scan to the required scale the detail will still be there. Such images are known as rastered images and are made up of tiny rectangles called pixels. Scanned artwork can rarely be used straight away as a decal because there will be too few pixels, resulting in a very grainy scan. Flood-filling and paintbrushing areas of solid colour, as well as other remedial tidying up can help, but the cleanest image will be what is called a 'vectored image'. Vectored images do not use pixels and are thus cleaner images. They can be made into rastered images if imported into a photo suite for artistic work, but they can also be printed direct from the art design software for a very clean image. Vectored images are made up of paths and anchor points. The path is the border of the various features of the design whilst the anchor points are small waypoint tools that can be manipulated to transform the design. Scanned in bitmap, or rastered, images can thus be traced over with paths to get a vectored copy, or object. Alternatively, designs can be made from scratch using the various tools on offer in the package you have. Most commercial decals are designed as vectored images in the latest version of the software packages mentioned earlier. These packages are in no way cheap and are really for the person who wants to make a living from designing vectored artwork.

CHAPTER 7

Weathering

Weathering, like most aspects of the final stages of scale aircraft modelling, is highly subjective. There is absolutely nothing wrong with giving your model a pristine finish, or even a high gloss finish if that is what you want. This tends to be referred to as the 'display finish', the emphasis being purely on the model as an aircraft. Many others prefer to finish their project in such a way that the emphasis lies more on the actual 'life' of the aircraft than in any aesthetic qualities that lie in the classic lines of the aircraft. This chapter is concerned more with the 'life' of the aircraft being represented.

Having decided to finish your model in a 'used' state, or for argument's sake say that the model in question is a military aircraft which you want to display in an operational state, the first step is to establish what the operational conditions for the aircraft were. In general, the main differences between military and civil aircraft are basically these – a civil aircraft has more turnaround time and has to look good for paying customers, whereas with military aircraft time is restricted to making the aircraft operationally reliable, full stop! All other issues with military aircraft are secondary.

HEAVY EROSION WEATHERING

Rough aerobatic handling, the ever-present threat of someone behind you who doesn't like you, different climates, soil composition, age of aircraft, maintenance conditions, parking, quality of paints used, broken or strained oil seals from tired, perhaps damaged engines,

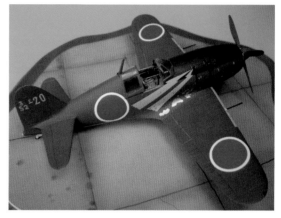

Weathering is an essential prerequisite to displaying 'in action' models effectively as it recreates the circumstances and environment of the original, be it the harsh paint-stripping climate of the Far East . . .

. . . or the war-weary existence of a post-war Mosquito.

Apart from the more familiar paints purchased from model shops, everything else comes from an art shop. Here we see such materials as Rowney oil paints and pastels, as well as a silver pencil made by Berol Verithin.

discoloured paintwork from angry exhaust manifolds, chips, scratches and dents caused by feet, hands, tools and pebbles and so on – these are all considerations and realities that play their part in determining just what an operational military aircraft will look like. So many variables are the reason why this stage of the modelling process is so subjective. One way to avoid overdoing weathering, which is always a concern, is to restrict yourself only to modelling a subject in the markings of an aircraft of which you have actual photos. This can be a real help in understanding the field conditions, so to speak, of your subject, although whilst it is historically beneficial, it is perhaps far too restrictive for most modellers. Nevertheless, reference photos can and should play a big part in how you proceed.

Probably one of the most distinctive weathering situations has to be that suffered by Japanese aircraft in WWII where both the weather conditions and poor quality of paint, as well as the poor, or non-existent, preparation of the bare metal underneath (mostly on the upper surfaces of Japanese aircraft) all contributed to even fairly new aircraft looking much the worse for wear. Recreating the look of an aircraft suffering from its upper camouflage

simply flaking off is a real challenge, especially in the smaller scales. It really is a question of what works the best? Painting metallic paint on top of the camouflage always looks just that, whereas scraping the camouflage paint away from a pre-painted bare metal undersurface is not only highly risky and can easily take up the metallic paint as well. It can also leave a step in the paintwork that will look out of scale. In a sense, the two greatest causes for why the paint came off are probably the answer from a modelling point of view. Paint came off because of poorly prepared undersurfaces; applying the same principle in modelling terms calls for the model to be pre-painted in a bare metal finish and then to have certain areas of that bare metal finish treated in such a way that they become bad hosts for subsequent layers of paint. Wet salt is perfect for this and can be positioned relatively well, although it is best on flat surfaces. Spraying the topcoat on whilst the salt is still wet will help to keep the salt in position. Both acrylic and enamel paints can be used with this method. Another excellent material to prepare the metallic surface prior to the camouflage painting is the sliver leaf 'rub and buff' system by the company Amaco, used in conjunction with acrylic paints like those in the excellent PolyScale range. The silver leaf is polished into the area where you want the paint to come off easily and acts as a barrier; the model is then sprayed with acrylic paint. Using a small cocktail stick, the acrylic paint can, when dry, be persuaded to exit the stage with very pleasing results in all scales. Be aware that the acrylic paint will not come off easily if the Amaco cream has been buffed into the Alclad II surface too well.

Another factor in the paint falling off is due to it being 'attacked' by the high levels of humidity common to East Asia. This factor can be manipulated for our modelling needs thanks to the availability of the bare metal paint range from Alclad II, which is highly resistant to solvent attack. As before, the model is pre-painted with a bare metal undersurface finish to which a camouflaged top coat of enamel paint is then applied. When thoroughly cured, cellulose solvent is applied in small amounts to the areas where you want the upper surface camouflage to be attacked. Be careful how much cellulose you apply: too much risks cutting through the Alclad, which, although resistant, is not immune. You also risk creating too large a patch of bare metal that may look unrealistic. Within a very short space of time even the smallest amount of cellulose will cause the enamel paint to blister up. The blistered paint can then be removed by applying the reverse side of Tamiya masking tape to it and gently pulling it off. Only the enamel paint that blistered up will pull off, leaving a very negligible step but creating some interesting and lifelike nonconformist shapes.

LIGHTER EROSION WEATHERING

For imitating the more common types of weathering found on operational aircraft we turn to perhaps more subtle means and methods. Staying for a moment with factors that attack paint, the most common observation will be of damaged paintwork from tools, footwear and churned-up stones. This can be easily mimicked with the judicious use of an artist's silver pencil. I say 'judicious', as the very reason for the damaged paint

denotes it is to be found in areas where maintenance work is often carried out and where the propeller directs the airflow laced with debris! Another consideration is the material being weathered. Is it metal? A de Havilland Mosquito 'Wooden Wonder' in temperate camouflage has not first been

Perhaps the most obvious technique in trying to recreate paint flaking is to take a scalpel blade to it. The technique is not bad as far as looks go if you remember to vary the direction of your scrapes, but it is very easy to go through the metal undercoat to the bare plastic.

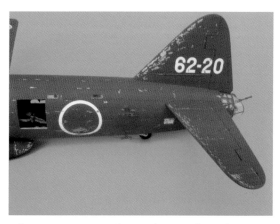

The paint-scraping technique has one clear advantage over other techniques . . . it can represent paint stripped from water-slide decal markings very well. Although it has to be said that paint flaking from the Japanese Hinomaru insignia was rare, being of much better paint and primer, the point remains as to the advantage of the technique.

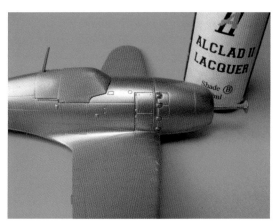

The first step in modelling a subject with noticeable paint flaking is to spray on a few coats of Alclad II Duralumin to act as a very tough base.

With the Alclad II base over-sprayed in Xtracolor enamel paint (when dry), a small amount of cellulose solvent is carefully applied with a brush to the areas where the paint is to be flaked.

The effect given by this technique in 1/72 is very pleasing as there is minimal step between the exposed bare metal Alclad II paint and the upper enamel camouflage.

This will blister up the enamel paint . . .

. . . which can then be pulled off with Tamiya masking tape.

sprayed aluminium dope so discretion is needed as to where any silver pencil can be applied. Likewise, it would be foolish to scratch away at a Ju 88, He 111 or Fw 190D-9 large composite propeller when the original is made of wood with a fabric covering.

STAINING

We now come to what we could consider to be the weathering techniques of 'staining' rather than 'eroding,' perhaps the most noticeable and notorious of which is exhaust staining. Much here depends in real life upon the maintenance of the engine, the quality of the fuel and oils being used and simply when the ground crew last got a chance to give the aircraft a good clean. It is a real eye-opener being at an air show and seeing ground crew with heavy duty brooms and buckets of detergent unceremoni-ously scrubbing exhaust staining off the aircraft. Again, much of what you do will, or should be, dictated by your reference material if your aim is to produce a scale replica of an operational machine. It will be noted that on light-coloured paintwork, like that found on mid-to-late WWII Luftwaffe nightfighters, the exhaust staining, compound-ed by poor-quality synthetic oils, is almost

The silver pencil is a great way to apply small paint chips and scratches. Here the Hasegawa 1/72 Raiden (given the designation 'Jack' by the US armed forces) is having scratches applied in conjunction with the more serious paint erosion already mentioned.

Here the silver pencil has been used most effectively to simulate the wear and tear experienced by the cockpit sill of the Hasegawa 1/32 Bf 109G-6.

The amount of scratches desired can eventually be built up to almost obscure the original paint in some places. A close inspection of wartime photographs of the type being modelled is always the best approach.

pitch black. On dark-coloured camouflage, such as the RAF's use of Night Black, the staining can take on hues of pink and light grey. Much of advanced scale aircraft modelling is about 'intelligent' modelling and this applies even to the colour of the exhaust staining you apply. As far as the actual application itself goes, sprayed-on exhaust staining looks the best as it can be more uniform in its coverage. Whether using a number of browns and shades of black or just one colour, the paint is diluted considerably and sprayed at very low pressure evenly over the appropriate area with the needle set at medium aperture. This setting creates a wide but non-concentrated coverage of paint to make the area look grubby from previous excursions. The colour can then be intensified by either changing the consistency, or by keeping the original mix but with a narrow needle aperture and higher-pressure setting. This more intense application needs discrimination in order to build up the staining in the immediate airflow of the exhaust discharge.

Diluted artist's oil paints are a very helpful medium for running into panel lines in order to accentuate their detail. This must be done sparingly and with consideration to scale. Too concentrated a mix of too dark a colour will do more damage to the aim of the exercise. If black must be used it is best to reserve it for running into the join detail of control surfaces to highlight their function. The above work is best done whilst the model is in a gloss state. The gloss surface enables the oil paint to run into the panel lines in a freer manner. It also aids cleaning up, as a cloth, slightly moistened with white spirit, will travel more freely over the surface of the model than if it was in a matt state. There are exceptions to the rule, however, as sometimes the 'soaking-in' effect of applying artist's oils to a matt surface will give just the result you are looking for. This can be

Sprayed-on diluted mixes of browns, blacks and greys with the careful use of the airbrush and little pressure is a great way of representing exhaust staining. It is easy to overdo this stage of the modelling process and consultation with references showing the real aircraft in real circumstances will help. Here the Airfix 1/48 Mosquito NF.30 operated by the Belgian Air Force after World War II looked decidedly grubby in the photograph, so it got more spray than normal.

This Hasegawa 1/32 Bf 109G-6 Messerschmitt flown by the Finnish Air Force got off more lightly to simulate a rather well-cared-for machine; note the airflow of the staining in the slipstream of the airscrew.

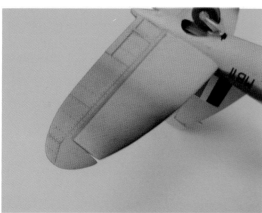

By using a very weak mix and low pressure to spray, the same colour can be slowly built up by spraying in one area more than another. Here the lower surfaces of the Mosquito's horizontal stabilizers have had the general airflow area slightly sprayed over with mucky black/brown but have had subsequent applications just hitting the leading edge of the stabilizer to depict a process in the build-up of staining.

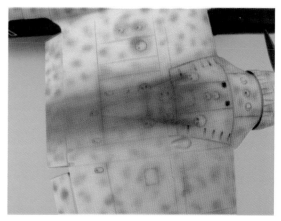

The same principle is seen here applied to a Revell 1/72 He 177A-3, but with a spray of Dark Earth applied first instead of a weak light coat of mucky black/brown to simulate previous attempts to clean the aircraft up. A further application of a darker mix in certain areas shows the dirt building up again.

appreciated in such areas as control surface hinges, where the spreading out and soaking-in effect of the diluted oil paint onto the matt surface around the hinge is perfect. As well as applying the oil from a brush in capillary fashion, it can also be applied to certain parts of

the aircraft by flicking the brush, thereby creating realistic splatter effects. However, be aware of two dangers when using diluted oil paints:

1. If the decals have been applied to the gloss

surface of the model before the oil paint is run into the panel lines, make sure that they have been well sealed in, using either Johnson's Clear floor polish or a sprayed coat of either acrylic or enamel gloss varnish. If the decals have not been sealed, when it comes to removing excess oil paint, you may inadvertently cause some of the waste to creep under the carrier film of the decal. If you do not want to take the time to seal in the decals, make sure you always wipe the residual oil paint away from the markings or apply the decals afterwards, being careful with an additional application of oil paints to pick out the now covered panel line without the need for too much cleaning up afterwards (alternatively, you can just use a little pastel as described below).

2. Do not think that just because you will be removing the waste you can slap on the oil paint. This will require more white spirit to remove it, risking cutting into the paintwork with this mild but potentially destructive solvent.

USING PASTELS

The final medium that we must give attention to in the execution of the stated aim of achieving a model aircraft which looks operational or alive, is that of artist's pastels. These most messy of materials are best kept in a secure environment, like a small sealable tub, as the dust can go everywhere! Their application demands that a small amount of the chosen colour be ground down by rubbing the block across some rough abrasive paper. This too is kept in the sealable tub. Make sure you wash your hands after this or you will get your fingerprints all over the model. A small, soft, cropped brush is an excellent tool for picking up small amounts of pastel powder from inside the tub, and depositing it on the aircraft, either with the full face of the brush for larger deposits, or with the edge of the face for finer applications. This work is best done on a matt surface, although there can be exceptions, as on a gloss surface wet pastel can be made to simulate oil streaks very effectively (or even the grain of a plywood surface as on the fuselage of an Albatros DV).

It has already been mentioned that the use of

Where the oil thrown out from an airscrew would hit the fuselage of the aircraft type, like in the case of the de Havilland Mosquito, a brush laden with diluted artist's oil paints, like raw umber, can be held next to the area in one hand whilst the other hand flicks the metal shaft. The splatter effect can be varied depending upon how diluted the oil paint is and whether the surface is matt or gloss.

solid black oil paint to accentuate panel/control surface detail can often rob the aircraft detail of its scale. Soft tones of dark brown pastel very slightly applied with the edge of the brush over such benighted panels can deintensify the whole situation remarkably. The only difficulty is that most browns disappear when sealed over with a coat of matt varnish. Nevertheless, if you feel the model will not come in for too much handling, then brown pastels offer very subtle weathering on their own as well as helping other media. Although not perfect for exhaust staining, when accompanied by sprayed-on staining, pastels, especially black, can be very useful for darkening panel lines caught in the wake of the exhaust blast.

Perhaps the best and most used application of this medium is for simulating the carbon staining present on aircraft that have fired their guns. Like with most other aspects of advanced

modelling, your references will be the best teachers in how to apply such staining. Much will depend on the calibre of weapon fired and the airflow particular to that aircraft type. If the aircraft is at readiness for another combat patrol but has not been washed from the last excursion, then it will have newly doped weapon aperture patches over the remnants of previous patches as well as previous staining.

You will hardly ever need to apply all of the

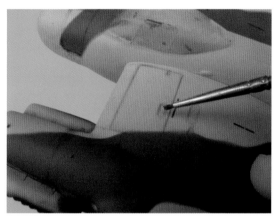

Pastels are also excellent at picking out any raised detail that you might want to keep.

Artist's oil paint can also be run into recessed detail. This can look a little too stark, especially if you have used a solid black wash. It can also spoil the scale! Unless it is a working or removable part, most other join lines in the aircraft's construction are actually filled in with putty to help airflow and increase speed. Whilst the modern tendency to have kits with recessed panel lines looks good, filling them with black ink, especially in smaller scales, can ruin the scale of the model. Where there may be a danger of this, soft brown artist's pastels can be used to deintensify the panel line by going over them with a pastel-laden brush.

Lighter shades of pastels can be used to simulate the grey exhaust staining seen on many British and American combat aircraft. These shades of pastel, however, just vanish when a protective seal of matt varnish is applied. The only answer is not to seal this kind of staining.

Mixes of various shades of artist's pastels can be used to simulate exhaust staining as seen here on this Ju 88A-1, but it is hard to apply the pastel as evenly as you would like.

After exhaust staining the most common discolouring of a combat aircraft will be around its gun ports and cartridge chutes due to carbon discharge from the exploding percussion caps. With great care these effects can be represented with sprayed paint but pastel offers much more control. Note how much muck four 20mm Hispano cannons chuck out . . .

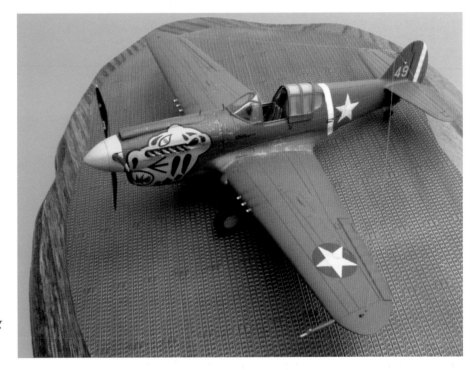

. . . compared with the much lighter ordnance of this P-40 with just a hint of pastel representing the carbon staining.

One final weathering technique has more to do with the subject of painting in Chapter 5, but, nevertheless, the pre-shading of panel lines, the use of a different shade of Olive Drab on the fabric control surfaces and a new panel here and there, plus the inclusion of a replacement landing flap showing a Medium Green mottle all go towards the weathered look on this 1/72 Italeri B-25.

above elements of weathering together on one model, but applying some of them will help to generate an atmosphere to your model that testifies to the circumstances in which the original was flown by brave men and women. It is highly recommended that you practise these techniques on a scrap model and not on your latest creation.

CHAPTER 8

Battle Damage

From time to time the mood may take you to display your model in such a state as to capture the reality of an 'operational' aircraft. In combat, the guy in the other uniform is trying to knock you out of the sky before you do the same to him – it really is as simple as that! In the process of achieving this objective, rifle calibre and possibly cannon ordnance are going to be converging as accurately as possible on the intended victim. Armour-piercing shells will cut through whatever is in their path until either passing right through or ricocheting around, causing yet more damage until utterly spent. High-explosive shells will simply detonate on impact to knock out vital control features. No matter what the size and type of the projectile it will leave both an entry wound and an exit wound, the latter being the most devastating. Such is the reality of air combat.

When choosing to model the realities of war in such a graphic manner the most crucial question to ask is: Would the aircraft have been able to get back to base for a wheels-down landing? The most obvious answer from a modelling point of view is only to model a subject for which you have photographic evidence. The question, however, remains an interesting one mechanically. The Spitfire Mk IIb modelled for this chapter had some five cannon shell hits amongst the numerous rifle calibre strikes and yet got home, whereas the photographs of Lt Nibel's Fw 190D-9 on the morning of 1 January 1945 during the Luftwaffe's costly *Operation Bodenplatte* show that the aircraft was brought down by a single

The impetus for a battle-damage project – some good photographs and an aftermarket decal option! Note how much damage was done by shell fire to the Spitfire Mk II's tail surfaces. It's a wonder that Sgt Marcin Machowiak of No. 306 (Polish) Squadron got back to terra firma.

bird strike to the radiator! Such are the fortunes of war, but it just proves that battle damage is something that must be modelled intelligently.

Once you have decided what to model and have a clear idea of what damage has been caused and whether or not the aircraft is going to need to lay wheels up on a permanent (appropriately detailed) base, the next question concerns how to represent the scale damage. Much depends on where the damage is, of course, and whether or not the blast has gone through numerous layers of structure. This latter damage can be a problem as both the sheet metal that has been blown in and the

Fw 190D-9 'Black 12' was flown and subsequently belly landed at Wemmel in Belgium on 1 January 1945 during Operation Bodenplatte *by Lt Theo Nibel of 10./JG 54. (Photo courtesy of Philip Evans)*

The reason . . . a small bird strike on the left half of the radiator! (Photo courtesy of Philip Evans)

structure that has been blown out need to be thin enough to be in scale, but also thick enough to keep some structural integrity. Aluminium kitchen foil is a great medium for accurately representing torn and shattered sheet metal in 1/72 scale, but is terrible at keeping its structural integrity.

The process starts with taking an impression of any kit detail to be replaced by tin foil. The tin foil is so thin that when rubbed over with a Q-tip every detail is shown. This detail is then cut out with a scalpel blade. As the tin foil has little strength of its own, the bare minimum of the kit area in question is cut away. The tin foil that has been previously cut to size is then grafted to the external damaged surfaces of the kit using a varnish or proper tin-foil glue by Microscale. Whatever glue you use, it is imperative that no extra thickness be given to the tin-foil panels so that they stand proud of the rest of the uncovered panels. With the tin-foil panels glued and layered over the kit, the Q-tip is once more applied to make sure no air is trapped under the surface and also to make sure that the tin foil has been measured correctly and lines up perfectly with the surrounding panel lines. However, no pressure must be put on the tin foil covering the holes cut into the plastic kit or it will depress and give a sharp edge to where the plastic underneath falls away. This must be avoided if the panel is to look realistic.

No other work is done now until after the model is all but finished. Be careful with any masking during the painting stage, as paint and primer will pull up easily from those surfaces where there is tin foil underneath. With the model decaled and coated in matt varnish the task at hand is to cut into the tin-foiled areas and carefully arrange the shattered panels to best represent the photographic evidence you have. It is a real temptation to go overboard here, but that would ruin everything you have worked for – better to understate than over-state. As with most aspects of this hobby, time

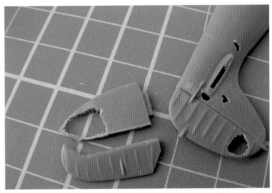

A certain amount of drilling out needs to be done with the hobby drill to aid the perception of the broken skins being hollow underneath.

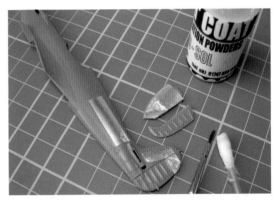

Using either the proper adhesive produced by the Bare Metal Foil Company, or a thin varnish like that used in the Hair-Coat system by the Small Shop EU (see Chapter 1), the replacement tin-foil skins are attached, being careful not to rub down where no plastic exists underneath.

Tin foil takes such good impressions that it is a relatively simple matter to cut out the correct sizes of replacement panels/skins.

needs to be taken. The work is completed by seeing to it that any bare tin foil showing that needs to be either lacquered or painted to represent doped linen is duly painted.

This has been an exercise to represent quite compact damage in a small scale; more extensive damage caused by an external explosion from anti-aircraft artillery would no doubt reveal more of the internal structure. It is hoped that working from photographs, taking the points and materials found in Chapter 1 as well as those in this chapter, will help you to accomplish realistic larger-scale battle damage.

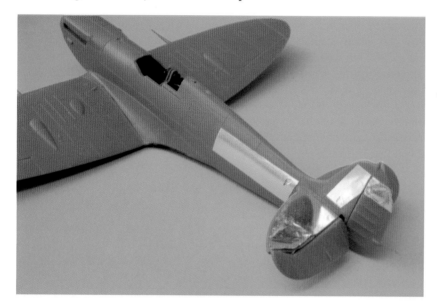

Using an adhesive as thin as varnish means that the wafer-thin foil sections hardly stand proud at all from their surroundings.

With close inspection of the reference photographs the tin foil can be sliced into and contorted to represent the effects of the hostile engagement.

Make sure that if you are representing battle damage to a doped fabric surface that you paint the reverse of the tin foil the appropriate colour!

It is important to realize that cannon and bullet shells have two effects, that which they create on entry and that which they create on exit. Here a cannon shell entering from above the left horizontal stabilizer has effectively blown out half the lower skin of the said stabilizer.

You might not want to make too many of your models like this, but such projects do bring home the awful reality of the subject, which is a sobering and helpful contemplation.

CHAPTER 9

Conversion Modelling

One of the key character traits of this hobby has to be 'individuality'. The difficulty comes in being able to display that sense of individuality when you know that what you are making is but one of thousands of kits produced by a mainstream kit manufacturer with good but limited decal options. For many modellers the answer will be simply to purchase an after-market decal sheet to multiply the marking and colour scheme options and thus gain that coveted quest for uniqueness. Still others will open the kit box and immediately see the possibilities to make it into a sub-type of that particular aircraft and thus force their individuality on the model that way. The motivation to make a model just that little bit different to what was intended by the manufacturer is also fuelled by a love for the history of the subject that this level of modelling naturally generates. Mainstream kit manufacturers cannot afford to release sub-types of a particular aircraft and so miss out important periods of aviation history. Instead, kits are restricted to perhaps one or two of the most numerous production variants. Over time, the range might increase to include other sub-types, but these are normally restricted to projects where the manufacturer can get away with an extra sprue of parts and a change in decal options. It is these restrictions that gave birth to aftermarket conversion sets.

There are and have been some very good aftermarket cottage industries, which for many years now have done all they can to provide good-quality and interesting conversion sets. The subject matter available is extensive, which

is not surprising – if the basic aircraft is good it is likely to stay in service a long time, so the greater the amount of variations. With a huge amount of potential subject matter at hand cottage industries set about their work to provide the modeller with the necessary conversion sets designed to fit particular kits. Some of these sets are extremely compre-

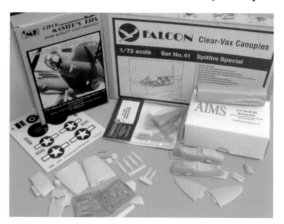

Some old and some new names in this area of the hobby. Falcon Industries have provided the impetuous for years with the offer of not only excellent direct replacement canopies but many conversion projects as well. With names like Paragon (sadly not trading at present) and Airwaves, probably more conversion sets have been designed for the Mosquito and the Spitfire than any other aircraft type. Most sets predominantly comprise polyurethane resin parts. Some include photo-etched brass vac-form canopies and white-metal parts, but very few conversion sets push the boat out as far as the CMK set shown which provides decals as well.

hensive, whilst others leave some homework for the modeller. Other sets are more mixed-media than others, that is to say some will be made up purely of resin parts, whilst others will have photo-etched brass, white-metal or clear vac-form parts, or even decal options in them as well. It has to be said that purchasing a set with decal options is very rare, as the cost of the printing and the perhaps limited appeal of the subject matter are at odds with each other. In saying that, it is wonderful to come across sets that cover everything – even at a price.

From time to time the mainstream manufacturers will get around to bringing out a kit that replaces a cottage-industry product. Another nail in the coffin comes from the cottage industry itself, as the longevity of the aftermarket conversion set can never be determined or guaranteed due to the domestic arrangements of the people involved. Other aftermarket conversion sets become unavailable because they are not selling. These sets only exist because a particular kit came on to the

market and a conversion set was designed to fit that particular model. If that model becomes unavailable, sales of the conversion set designed for it dry up. If you see a conversion set available, and you are sure you would like to get around to making it one day – buy it there and then! As has been pointed out already conversion sets are based on a particular model. Kits of the same aircraft but by a different manufacturer can be used, but the project proceeds at the modeller's own risk as discrepancies between kits of the same aircraft abound. It is

White-metal parts found in conversion sets are like all other dissimilar materials in modelling – superglue or speed epoxy are the only answer to their being secured in place.

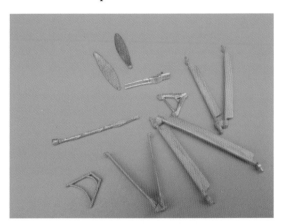

Where parts are needed that are difficult to cast in resin, even with a degassing or vacuum-chamber, having a white-metal mould made is often the only answer. These are by no means cheap and put the price up to the customer somewhat, due to the expense of the mould, cost of the material and the fact that the manufacturer will want to produce a minimum of twenty runs for you to make it worth their while. It is worth considering all of this when you are wondering about the price of the conversion set.

Different qualities of white-metal are available, but all benefit from cleaning up with wet and dry abrasive paper to delete slight imperfections in the surface; occasionally filler will be needed.

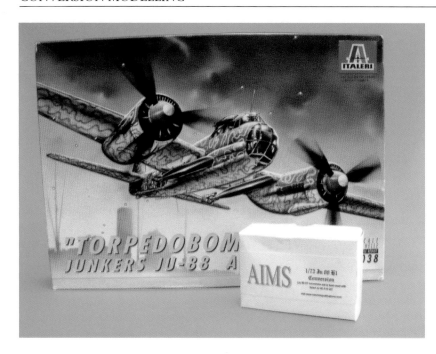

What Paragon did for the Mosquito, I am trying with my own AIMS sets to do for the Ju 88. In this case, it is a conversion project to turn either an Italeri 1/72 Ju 88A-4 or A-16 into a Ju 88H-1 variant by supplying resin, white-metal and vac-form items. Like many conversion sets, the injection-moulded manufacturers eventually catch up and make sets like this less viable.

always safer to use the kit that the conversion set says it is designed for.

Probably the most significant feature of the whole conversion modelling procedure is the initial surgical stage. Some conversion sets provide parts that just replace kit parts, such as the engines. This is still conversion modelling, but can best be described as micro-conversion. The majority of conversion sets, however, deal with sub-types that are quite different from those released by the mainstream kit manufacturer, which means getting the razor saw out, the end result being – macro-conversion!

It is a good idea to spend some extra time thinking about the project and identifying the areas of the kit that are to be surgically removed. There is no point rushing and ending up spoiling a perfectly good kit. Are you happy that the conversion set is accurate? Do you understand the instructions, which may not have that professionalism about them seen in mainstream instruction sheets? Can you begin, or are there other purchases to be made? Are there decals available for this project, or will you have to go to the spares box? Do you have any references for this machine, or are you

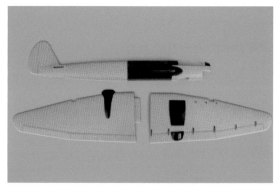

Conversion modelling inevitably requires various degrees of surgery. One help to making sure you remove the right areas is to black the unwanted areas out with a permanent pen. Following the instructions carefully, the unwanted plastic can then be removed using various kinds of hobby saw from companies like X-Acto.

relying solely on the instructions? Put another way, proceed in the same way as you would do for a mainstream injection-moulded kit, but perhaps a little slower due to the fact you are contemplating wrecking it!

Once convinced that you have identified

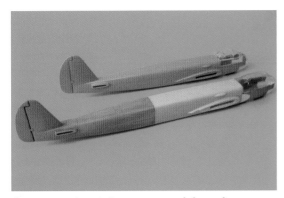

Some conversion projects are very subtle – others definitely are not, as seen here when the extended fuselage of the Ju 88H-1 conversion project is placed next to what the kit manufacturer (Italeri) intended!

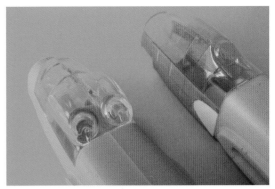

Some conversion sets provide replacement vac-form canopies, either because the replacement canopy is better quality than the kit part or because – as in this case – the conversion project necessitates it. The Ju 88H-1 has a different rear-defence set-up than the Ju 88A-4 canopy it replaces.

Not strictly conversion items, the rear gear bay nacelles are more 'correction items' (being much fatter than the kit parts), but as the front sections are needed to take the BMW 801D power plants instead of the kit's Jumo 211 anyway, the whole gear bay, forward and aft, may as well be provided to both convert and correct the kit in this

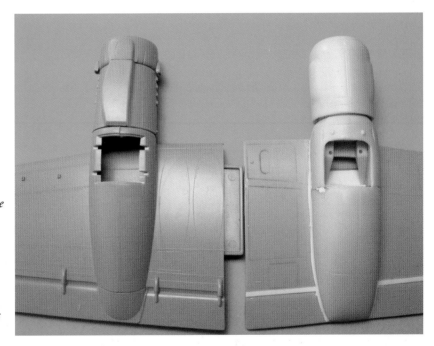

exactly where surgery needs to be executed, proceed with a good, firm hobby saw for straight line cuts and more flexible razor saws for all other work. Most conversion parts will be designed to meet the kit parts at a particular panel line. Therefore when this applies to fuselage parts, carve up your model in such a way as to leave the kit part that will be used again 0.5mm longer than it needs to be. This gives 0.5mm to trim back, play around with and adjust to get the best fit with the aftermarket part.

The use of the materials involved in these conversion sets has already been covered else-

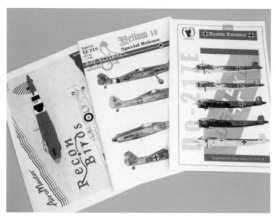

This photo illustrates three areas of small cottage industry products quite well. 1) The need for filler. These sets are produced by enthusiasts not trained engineers. 2) Various details, such as the camera ports in the aft fuselage belly, are researched and added by the modeller. Instructions provided in most conversion sets generally give you all the information you will need, but other sets will require the modeller to know the subject. 3) Occasionally it is impossible for the producer of the set to include all the detail that they would like to. Such missing detail (such as these FuG 200 aerial arrays by Kora) can be purchased elsewhere cheaper than if the producer of the conversion set had tried to provide similar examples.

Conversion modelling has been helped tremendously by the big boys in the decal industry including on their decal sheets subjects that require conversion work. It has already been inferred in the praise heaped upon CMK for producing a conversion set with decals that this is not the norm and that the modeller is left to hunt down the needed decals elsewhere.

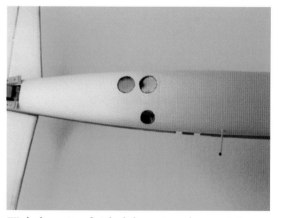

When no decals exist already on an aftermarket decal sheet the modeller has to either buy a number of decal sheets they think will help or hunt through their existing collection.

With the project finished the various characteristics of the converted model distinguish themselves, such as the replication of these three camera portholes, the Ju 88H-1 having primarily a long-range reconnaissance role with the 3rd Staffel of 120 Gruppe.

where in this book – such as in Chapter 3 where the spotlight is on working with polyurethane resin – so there is no need for repetition here. Everything depends on the preparation of the parts involved, but with careful sawing and perhaps just a little more filler than usual there is no reason why a conversion project should turn out any worse than a straight-from-the-box model. Indeed, it may turn out much better due to the extra concentration; and it will most definitely turn out unique.

A number of Luftwaffe machines experimented unsuccessfully with extra defence in the form of a couple of medium-calibre rear-firing machine guns. On the few Ju 88 C-7s built, and as here on one of the eight Ju 88H-1s built, these were housed in a small belly pod, whereas on the Dornier Do 217K-2 they were housed in the tail fairing.

Note the busy front end of the Ju 88H-1 with the excellent Kora FuG 200 anti-shipping dipoles and the canopy periscope present on all Luftwaffe types using rear-firing pilot-controlled weapons.

CROSS-KITTING

Another side to conversion modelling relies not on aftermarket conversion sets but upon cross-kitting. This is perhaps the older of the two means of producing a model that is different to the intentions of the manufacturer and only really takes place these days when the after-market equivalent is not available. Cross-kitting at one extreme can be very wasteful and expensive as a number of kits of the same type, but different sub-types, are grafted together to make a sub-type as yet unrepresented by both the mainstream manufacturers and the cottage industries. In reality, this kind of conversion modelling project is rare, it being much more likely that a number of kits would be grafted together to make one good example of the aircraft type. This is not strictly conversion modelling, but such a procedure belongs here more than anywhere else.

It is not just aircraft that can be cross-kitted, but their ancillaries as well. For example, cross-kitting the British Paveway II from the Airfix weapons set and the GBU 10 from the Hasegawa weapons set (with the help of filler and styrene

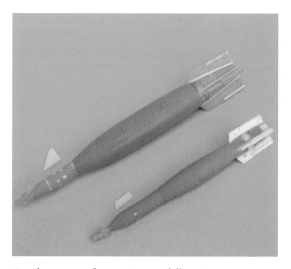

Another aspect of conversion modelling is 'cross-kitting.' Here the British Paveway Laser-Guided Bomb (LGB) from the 1/72 Airfix Weapons Set and the older-style American GBU 10 from the Hasegawa American Weapons Set have been grafted together (converted) to model a modern GBU 10 as used in Operation Desert Storm in 1991, and more recently in Operation Iraqi Freedom in 2003.

Placed alongside remodelled GBU 12s this converted GBU 10 ordnance looks the business on the F-15E Strike Eagle.

sheet) produces a fair representation of a modern GBU 10 as carried by the F-15E.

At the other end of the extreme, cross-kitting involves more swapping than sawing and can be as simple as taking the propeller from one kit to use on another. The best cross-kitting is where there is no waste at all, but this only really happens with kits where one of them has enough parts to offer a choice of options and where the use of these extra parts on another kit entails no other structural changes.

Here the faired-in dorsal and ventral gun positions of the Italeri 1/72 Do 217N-1 cunningly make it a Do 217N-2.

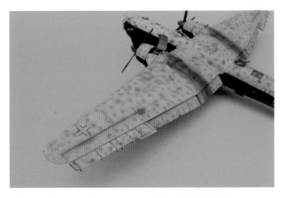

Here the split aileron set-up of the He 177A-3 converts without much fuss the Revell 1/72 He 177A-5 into an earlier type.

Here, however, the squared off wing tips, early rudder, early canopy and earlier Jumo 211 engines as found on the Ju 88A-1 give a quite different model from that intended by Italeri, but still the whole thing is hardly boisterous . . .

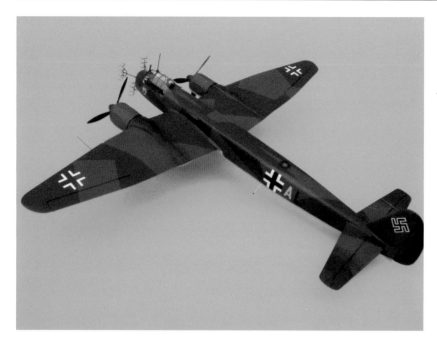

. . . unlike the Ju 88H-1 with its fuselage lengthened fore and aft of the wing root making for a decidedly odd-looking aircraft.

Unlike the slick lines of the Mosquito PR. 1 converted from the Tamiya Mosquito Mk IV using the Model Aeroplane Monthly 1/72 conversion set.

Most conversion projects are far subtler than the Ju 88H-1 project we have looked at. Here simply the absence of an aerial mast and the presence of an oblique camera turn a 1/72 Tamiya Spitfire Mk 1 into a Spitfire PR Type 1G (externally anyway)!

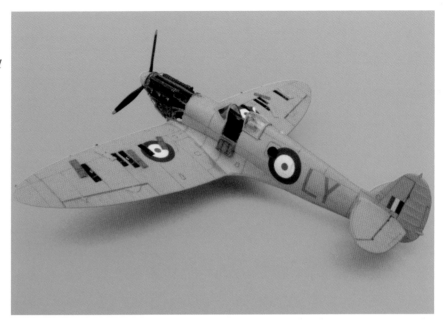

Much like the Ju 88H-1 project this Avro Shackleton MR II takes on a marked difference as it goes from being an MR III with tricycle undercarriage and tip tanks to a 'tail sitter' with rounded wing tips thanks to the most comprehensive Aeroclub conversion set for the Frog 1/72 Shackleton MR III (the author's first conversion project).

Even in 1/72 Andrew Eaton's B-52G is a 'monster', converted from the Monogram B-52D using the ED Models conversion set comprising new resin nose, engine fronts and side blisters and . . .

. . . a replacement section for the tail gunner's position.

CHAPTER 10

Vac-Form Biplane Modelling

When looking around a model show you will not fail to notice those fragile little 'string bags' that must stand in a class of their own, like their owners to whom you take off your hat and fancy that should you ever meet such an expert at the dizzying heights of our hobby you would be sure to burble out something foolish before retreating in shame, desiring that mercy be shown and you be given another chance to do better! Of course, it is not all as melodramatic as that, but the point is a valid one; biplane models are delicate and demanding aircraft that when made well take the breath away. In that sense, the subject rightly needs to be covered in a book with a title such as this one – but it is not all doom and gloom. It has to be remembered that there is a good chance that the show-stopping 'string bag' was made by someone who is intimately acquainted with this area of the hobby. They perhaps only do these kinds of model and will not blink an eyelid at the thought of only being able to finish one or two a year. They know every trick, every obscure retail outlet producing scale wicker seats and spoked wheels! They are able to make whole aircraft out of what looks like the original materials without thought to time or cost. Such people are indeed masters in their field and it would be unrealistic to try to copy them, for what they and we understand by 'advanced scale aircraft modelling' is quite different altogether.

For those of us who will wish to model a biplane only infrequently, this is 'advanced modelling' due to a number of factors: reference material might be hard to come by; we may

have failed on previous occasions to represent wood effect and rigging as well as we had hoped; the aircraft we wish to model may be in a more demanding medium that we have little experience of; or there may be deficiencies in the kit we have due to its limited nature. These, and perhaps other, reasons tend to make many of us shy away from this area of advanced scale aircraft modelling, but it is to our loss because there are some great biplane kits available, amongst them those of the vac-form variety.

Limited-run vac-form kits have something of the 'poor cousin' air about them, being cast in a rather dim light by the quality and ease of construction of the mainstream injection-moulded kits. Even polyurethane resin limited-run kits seem to come off better, and they are far more expensive. Is the poor reputation of these vac-form kits justified? And if not, why?

It has to be said that on opening the box two aspects of vac-form modelling are readily apparent:

1. The preparation stage of the build will be much longer and perhaps much more difficult.
2. Only the barest of non-vac-form details may have been provided in another medium like white metal. This means that in order to build this kit that the mainstream manu-facturers have not bothered about you will have to take your time. You will have to follow a number of proven steps so as not to make a mess of the preparation stage, you will definitely need to have access to

There are some lovely biplane models around in injection-moulded plastic, vac-form plastic and resin.

It is hard to ignore how attractive the subject of biplane modelling is, a fact attested to and promoted by the excellently informative and inspiring Osprey publications on many of the combat types in service during the most colourful period in aviation history – WWI.

They don't come too much brighter than the excellent decal options in Eduard's neat little 1/72 Albatros D.Va 'ProfiPack' kit, and therein is the appeal.

More generalized help on biplane modelling can be derived from both specific and general modelling magazines, as well as books portraying restored aircraft types.

LEFT: *Probably the biggest headache for modellers in love with biplane modelling – references. Relatively few vintage aircraft remain and specialist publications such as the Windsock Datafile series are invaluable to the modeller contemplating modelling a vintage biplane kit.*

reference material and finally you will need to be able to scratchbuild missing detail (*see* Chapter 1) and perhaps even design your own markings (*see* Chapter 6).

REFERENCE MATERIAL

Reference material is such a key factor in trying to improve your game, and no more so than when biplanes are involved. With all those rigging wires and control surface wires needing to run to and fro from the right places and those open cockpits (in the majority of cases), where in the case of a vac-form kit not much may presently exist, references are essential. What Falcon Industries have been to canopies, so Windsock have been to biplane modelling. Their magazines and more specific reference publications, namely their *Modellers Datafile* range, have imbued modellers with the confidence to build these classic aircraft.

Unfortunately, Windsock almost exclusively caters for military aircraft, which leaves only one option if no other modelling based publications are available: your own camera. Museums like the RAF Museum at Hendon, North London, and the Fleet Air Arm Museum at Yeovilton, Somerset, have some great static display examples, whereas a mix of civilian and military airworthy types can be found in the excellent Shuttleworth Collection in Bedfordshire. There is always the chance, however, that if the biplane you want to model is a civilian type, examples may be owned and flown in private collections at a nearby aerodrome. It will not hurt to phone up a number of airfields and flying schools in your area and ask if anyone keeps such and such there. Most likely they will be happy to put you in contact with the owner so that you can arrange a photo session; you may even get a flight, who knows?

The best reference source, however, will be your own camera, whether that entails a trip to somewhere like the Shuttleworth Collection or to a local aerodrome where a vintage aircraft is maintained and flown.

Take the opportunity to amass a virtual
Squadron/Signal Walk Around-style photo album,
taking in such details as the engine compartment . . .

. . . cockpit details . . .

. . . exhaust system . . .

. . . propeller wood colours . . .

. . . fuel lines . . .

. . . and control surface details.

PREPARATION

Marking Out

The first step in modelling vac-form kits is one of the most important – marking out. A clear distinction has to be made between what is kit and what is backing sheet. Whether a soft pencil or a permanent pen with very fine nib is used, it is essential to apply the mark at the very base of the vac-form kit part. There is of course a third way of creating the needed distinction and that is by priming the whole part and surrounding attached backing with primer (*see* Chapter 5).

With the kit parts clearly marked out and perhaps separated from the bulk of the vac-form sheet for better access all round, either a more sturdy blade like the X-Acto No. 2 or indeed a scribing instrument is applied to the base of the kit part and cut into at a 45-degree angle with medium pressure. Once all the parts have been separated they will be ready for trimming the angled remnants of the backing sheet aft of the distinguishing mark.

Sanding

Perhaps the greatest difficulty faced in the entire preparation stage is that which comes next – sanding away the left-over backing sheet without either going too far or sanding away the tips of your fingers! Aeroclub have come to the rescue here with the sale of small, extremely robust double-sided sticky tabs. Until recently, they also sold a small T-shaped handle as well, the idea being that you have a tool that can both be held onto comfortably during the sanding process and will also take the sticky pads (across the top of the T). This product is now discontinued, but the concept is ideal. Other items lying around the house or garage will do equally well, such as a small doorknob or a length of 1in by 0.5in beading. Eighty (80) grit abrasive paper taped securely onto a waterproof surface, like an offcut of Pharmacia board, offers the best sanding platform. Make sure that one side of the abrasive paper follows the edge of the board. Much depends on the size and shape of the object as to how one

The fine detail might be absent and the instructions limited in what are called 'limited-run' kits, like this Aeroclub 1/48 de Havilland DH 60G Moth vac-form kit, but ignoring the extra work presented by this kind of kit for a moment you will notice that you have the makings of a lovely model that is probably not available in any other medium.

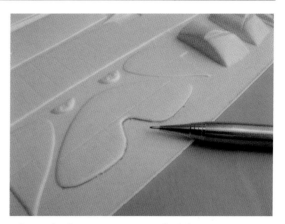

The work of constructing a vac-form kit may seem daunting but it is not really. It begins with marking out the parts to be separated from the vac-form backing sheet with either a pencil . . .

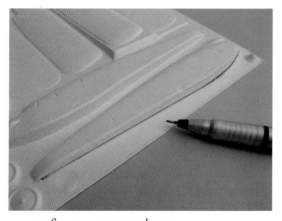

. . . or a fine permanent marker pen.

Another way of marking out the parts prior to separation is to prime them (see *Chapter 5*).

decides the best way to sand it down, but most objects are done in the centre of the sheet of abrasive paper with plenty of water, the exception being the wings. Because sanding the whole wing section at the same time, so that the leading and trailing edge of the wing are simultaneously in contact with the abrasive paper, will spoil the aerofoil by taking too much off the leading edge, it is best to complete the sanding process in smaller stages. This is best done by sanding the leading edge followed by the trailing edge using the abrasive paper at the edge of the Pharmacia board. Even with this precautionary measure it is still easy to make mistakes, as during the trimming down of the trailing edges of the wings it is too easy to lift the angle of sanding slightly. The result will then be that when you place the wing half on a flat surface there will be shadow underneath the trailing edge that should not be there. Scraping

A sturdy blade is then used to score gently around the base of the mark at a 45-degree angle a number of times until the part can be easily snapped off from the backing sheet.

The same work can be done with a fine scribing instrument.

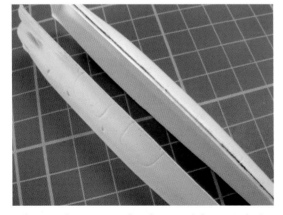

Whatever the means used to distinguish between the kit part and the leftover thickness of the backing sheet, the key thing is that you can clearly see the difference.

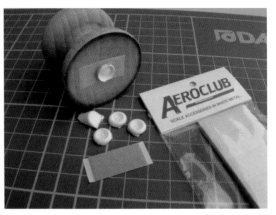

The second stage of preparing vac-form model parts for construction is the sanding down of the leftover backing sheet at the base of each part. Aeroclub very helpfully produce small high-tack double-sided tabs to help secure the small parts to a handy object like this small drawer handle . . .

. . . or larger objects like this fuselage to a length of 2.5 × 1cm wide wood.

away the plastic on the reverse face up to the edge of the trailing edge with a round X-Acto No. 10 blade will rectify this unfortunate error. Whatever you are sanding, to quote John Adams of Aeroclub, "The black line is king." Whatever you do, trust the mark that you placed onto the kit parts before cutting them out and stop sanding when you reach it.

Making Locating Tabs

All of the above work is endemic to this kind of kit, and only brings you to a point where you

Helped by the Aeroclub sticky tabs, small parts can be easily sanded down using a circular motion on top of wet and dry abrasive paper (80 grit) secured in place on a water-resistant board such as Pharmacia.

Larger objects are done in much the same way, but it may prove easier to grind the item forwards and backwards.

One of the hardest areas of a vac-form model to prepare is the wings. Sanding both the leading and trailing edges at the same time is sure to take too much plastic off the leading edge, so the best way to tackle the problem is to do the wing in eight stages.

There is a real tendency when sanding wings to lift the wing slightly so that you are sanding at an angle. You can tell you have done this when you place the wing half on a flat surface and there is a shadow underneath the trailing edge. A curved No. 10 X-Acto hobby blade scraped along the inside edge of the wing will help reduce this quite easily.

have the kit parts to work with as you would with an injection-moulded kit, once you had cut them off the sprue. With the vac-form variety of kit there are still further preparations to be made, as, unlike the injection-moulded kits, vac-form kit parts (and polyurethane resin kit parts) have no inherent means of being

secured other than by butting them up against each other, which provides no foundation to the join. This calls for locating tabs to be cemented into the fusclage spine and floor with offcuts of either the backing sheet or Evergreen plastic sheet. This will help the fuselage halves to line up, as well as giving the halves further

113

surfaces to which to bond, providing a much more stable object to fill and sand down (if such work is required). Lengths of brass rod are also needed both to pin the lower wing to the fuselage and to fix the aerofoil-shaped interplane struts in place on the lower wings and fuselage. Careful drilling is required, both to the tips of the sections of struts and to their wing location points. Indeed, it is probably best to drill such holes in the appropriate wing skin before the two halves are cemented together, thus preventing drilling through the soft plastic of both halves by mistake.

Before we move onto construction, in case you were wondering why vac-form models have lots of small nodules covering the kit parts it is because such vac-form kits are produced using a female-type mould. To help the hot plastic to be sucked down into the female mould more effectively, small air holes are drilled at strategic intervals all over the mould, resulting in lots of small nodules over the surface of the kit that need to be removed.

CONSTRUCTION

Making a Jig

Although not essential, it is advisable at some stage before the lower wings are attached to

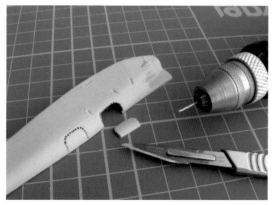

Removing plastic from where apertures should be is a simple matter with a hobby drill. The plastic is soft, so not much pressure will be needed nor many revolutions on the transformer. A No. 11 Swann-Morton scalpel blade follows up the work excellently.

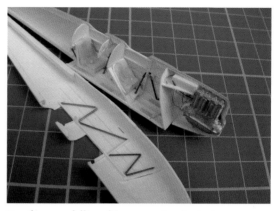

Vac-form modelling, like most other limited-run media, relies heavily on other disciplines, for example internal scratchbuilding using materials such as Evergreen plastic sheet and strip, brass rod, Tamiya masking tape, wire, and even Plasticilin mounting wax covered in PVA wood glue for the seat cushions.

make a jig based on the plans provided in the instruction sheet. Due to the relatively delicate nature of biplanes and the need to use superglue on the brass locating pins, the jig, be it an elaborate affair or not, helps to keep the various features of the aircraft at the right angles whilst the glue is setting. A cheap, easy to cut, but sturdy enough material like artist's board (used to frame pictures) makes an ideal jig. Smaller offcuts form the fuselage and wing supports. A central line is first drawn on the base. A mark on the centre line then indicates where the first fuselage support is to sit, the set square being used either side of the centre line to make sure the support will sit at the right angle. The next mark on the centre line is for the leading edge of the wing. This is measured back precisely from where the first mark is located. If this is not accomplished the height of the wing supports may be wrong, giving either too much or too little dihedral. Again, the set square is used, in conjunction with the overhead scale plans of the wings, to mark out the best place for the wing supports. It goes without saying that wings that are not swept back are much easier to plan to. The final mark on the centre line is for the rear of the fuselage

Clear-part modelling also plays a part when it comes to needing to replicate instrument dials. Black acrylic paint is painted onto one side of some acetate sheet. When dry, the black acrylic paint is scratched off to represent the various gauges and any writing. When the black paint is covered over with a coat of white paint (or a multitude of colours for that matter), and the acetate turned over, you have some great homemade instrument dials.

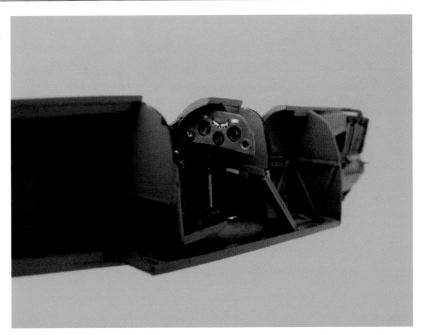

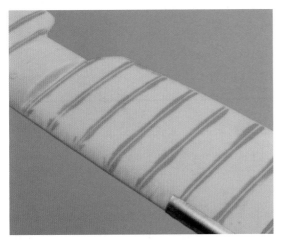

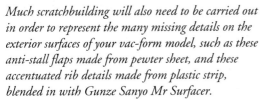

Much scratchbuilding will also need to be carried out in order to represent the many missing details on the exterior surfaces of your vac-form model, such as these anti-stall flaps made from pewter sheet, and these accentuated rib details made from plastic strip, blended in with Gunze Sanyo Mr Surfacer.

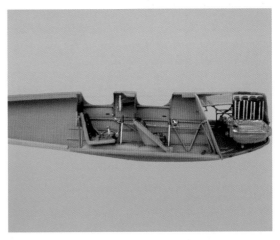

Like all projects, limited run or not, there comes a time when you can enjoy what you have accomplished, sometimes from next to nothing, before gluing the fuselage halves together. Note the increased depth of the fuselage thickness to get an even stronger join in the absence of locating pins as found on most injection-moulded kits.

and is again measured back precisely from the first mark so that the fuselage sits at the right height on the tail support. If the tail sits either too low or too high the angle of incidence on the lower wing will be affected. With the fuselage sat in place, the lower wings can be attached to the fuselage with brass pins, using superglue. The correct angle of incidence of the lower wings is achieved both by the correct sit of the fuselage and by the wing supports having

Due to the need to use superglue and pins to construct vac-form kits a jig is a very helpful tool to have. Scale plans (in this case supplied with the kit) are consulted to get the various measurements needed. The most important factor in designing a jig is consistency. All the measurements must be taken from a base line. Where scale plans are provided a ruler can be placed along the length of the datum line and a line drawn along the lower length of the ruler to form a base line. Using a set square, measurements are taken up from the base line to where they meet the fuselage and wings.

A cheap, easy to cut, but sturdy enough material like artist's board (as used to frame pictures) makes an ideal jig. Smaller offcuts form the fuselage and wing supports.

One area where brass pins definitely need to be located is in the otherwise flimsy Contrail interplane struts.

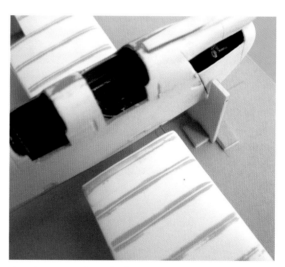

Another area where the brass pins are really helpful is in the locating, but not necessarily gluing, of the lower wings. With the fuselage sat in place on the jig the lower wings can be attached to the fuselage with considerable confidence as to the accuracy of their fit . . .

been measured and then cut at an angle so that the wing's leading edge sits taller than the trailing edge. Using a jig does of course open up the possibility of being able to paint and decal the model in sections before final assembly with brass pins and the jig, leaving only the rigging left to do where the vac-form project is a biplane.

. . . especially when the wing supports have been designed to take into consideration the angle of incidence of the lower wing as well.

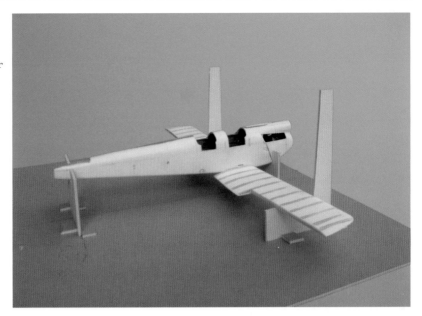

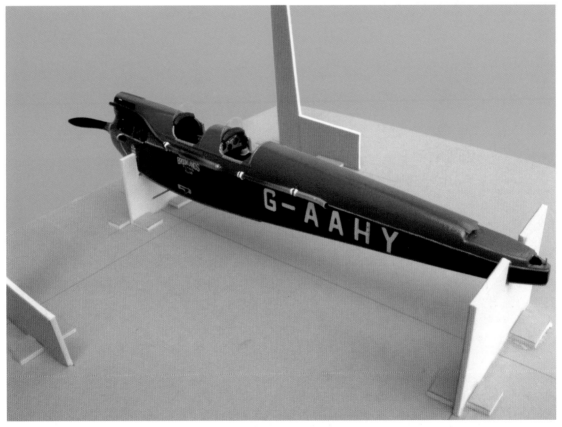

With such confidence generated by the jig's accuracy, whole sub-assemblies of the model can be virtually finished!

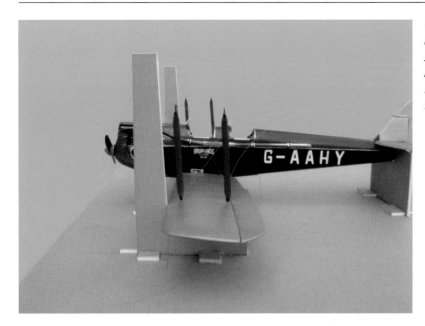

Other helpful features of the jig can be designed so as to help with the angle and pinning of the interplane struts mentioned earlier.

It is possible to overstress the wing when rigging. Rigging the model whilst on the jig gives you a constant visual reference point to help keep everything plumb.

Rigging

Thin metal wire, as used by railway modelling enthusiasts for wiring their points, at first appearances looks a simple way to rig a biplane, and looks very authentic if you use thin enough wire to complement the scale of the model, but there are many problems.

The lengths of wire are pulled from their protective sleeves, separated from each other and then rolled over with a steel rule to straighten them out. Trying to establish the precise measurements of the wires needed is quite tedious and with only the shallowest of pre-drilled pilot holes the actual gluing of them can be rather untidy, as more PVA wood glue or superglue is needed and it has nowhere to go except sit on the surface in a puddle.

Another downside of this style of post-build rigging is that it is not very strong and the attachment points can come away. The wire can also be bent, unlike materials used in other rigging techniques. Here some of the rigging from the 1/72 Tasman re-release of the Heller de Havilland Domini/Rapide has come away. If the lengths of rigging are too long the metal wires can also sag under their own weight.

Rigging *continued*

Depending on the damage, the rigging in question can either be replaced entirely (this really needs to be done if the metal wire has a kink in it), or carefully nurtured back into position and reattached.

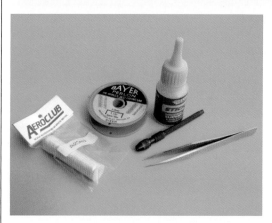

The other, and probably better, technique for rigging involves the threading of such materials as 1lb fishing wire, invisible mending thread and Lycra elastic thread (like that sold by Aeroclub). Superglue, good tweezers and a number of 0.3mm drill bits will be needed for this very strong and durable rigging technique.

Work commences with the drilling of the pilot holes at the bases of the various struts on the lower wing to accept the chosen flexible material, being careful not to drill all the way through. Be careful and check your references, as the distance between the strut and the tie rod differs between designs.

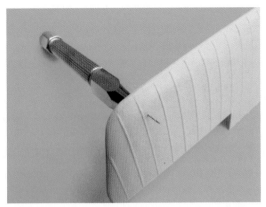

On the top wing, however, the holes are drilled all the way through. The work can obviously also be done in the reverse of these last two steps.

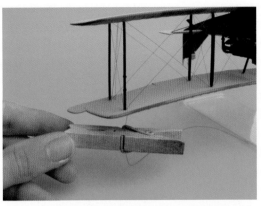

A good way to get sufficient tension in the rigging is to attach a weight to the waste rigging whilst the model is held upside down. The rigging is pulled back slightly, coated with superglue and then allowed to drop back through the pre-drilled hole under weight.

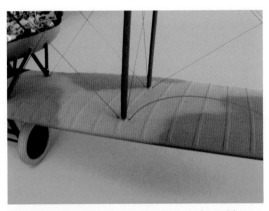

The rigging is anchored to the lower wing with a drop of superglue.

Once set, the waste rigging is sliced off as neatly as possible and the evidence of the wire concealed with a drop of superglue.

It is then fed through the upper wing with tweezers.

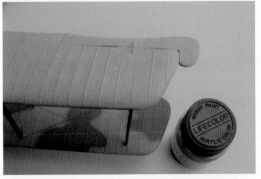

The super glue can then be sanded down and hand-painted over.

Rigging *continued*

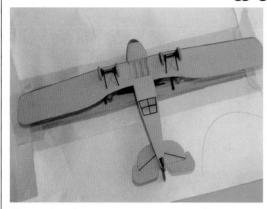

The upper wing can then be masked off from beneath ready for any airbrush work.

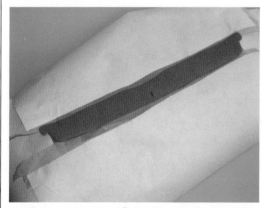

This effectively makes a masking tent.

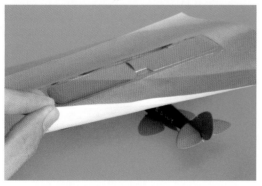

Of course, where the upper wing is one solid colour, and especially when that solid colour is metallic, it is best to avoid any hand painting and simply get on with masking ready for spraying the final area of your biplane.

Rigging, as found both in the internal construction of the fuselage and external support of the aircraft's main and tailplanes, consists of steel tie rods with adjustable ends. These adjustable steel wires give extra strength internally, being crossed over between the vertical and horizontal compression members, as well as externally on the tail surfaces and between the forward and aft interplane struts, both on the wing and the fuselage. Still further steel tie rods have a maintenance purpose, being strung between the outer and inner interplane struts to help to keep the correct dihedral and angle of incidence. The tie rods travelling down from the top of the inner interplane struts to the bottom of the outer struts are called 'landing wires', whereas the tie rods strung from the top of the outer interplane struts down to the lower wing root (where a single bay is concerned, that is only one set of wing struts) are called 'flying' or 'lift wires'. Where landing and lift wires cross they are held together by either small round devices called acorns or long cord-wise rods called tie bars. The various wires cut into the slots provided in either the acorn or tie bar and are held in place, thus preventing any sagging.

Unlike the tie rods with their sleek aerofoil steel coverings, control cables are lighter, unprotected steel twine objects that run from elevated clearance horns attached to the rudder and elevator down to the cockpit. Various designs of actuator, some external, some internal, work the ailerons by means of internal control cables fed back to the control column. Where the ailerons are situated on the lower wing the control cables can sometimes be seen protruding out of the wing root and into the belly of the cockpit to meet with the control column.

These then are the basics of vac-form biplane modelling preparation and construction, here explained specifically with reference to building a biplane. When accompanied by the much-needed scratchbuilding, and when realistically and strongly rigged (as demonstrated by Martin Hale's model in the box on 'Rigging'), you can end up with a delightful representation of a classic aircraft, limited in manufacture but certainly not limited in appeal. The project may take a bit longer than others due to the limitations of the medium being used and the subject being modelled, but with patience there is no reason why a vac-form model should not turn out just as good as a model in any other medium. Is therefore the general modelling public's shyness towards vac-form models understandable? The answer really has to be no! The only difference in the whole process, over against other styles of kit, is one of time and care. As the qualities of patience and attention to detail are so necessary in our hobby anyway, we should by no means pass up the opportunity to make a vac-form kit of an aircraft not represented in any other medium.

Detail shot of the finished model.

With the right references, a sensible approach to the construction and perhaps a little more patience you soon end up with a model just as good, if not better, than an injection-moulded kit that needed half the work.

Overview of the finished model.

Detail shot of the finished model.

Wood Effects

Models representing lacquered natural wood finishes are eye-catching to say the least, as Martin Hale's scratchbuilt 1/48 scale Felixstowe F.3 amply demonstrates. But how is it done?

A great way to start is by closely examining the real thing and taking note of how many shades of brown make up a compressed mahogany propeller . . .

RIGHT : . . . or even the lack of them in these spruce struts!

Wood Effects *continued*

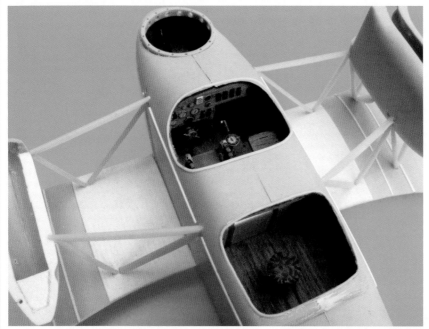

Trying to paint wood effect is not the only option available. Where flat surfaces are concerned, as on this 1/48 AEG IV's cockpit floor, Marketry Veneer can be used to simulate the wooden flooring very well. Marketry Veneer is available from craft and specialist doll's house shops.

Or what about purchasing handmade compressed and sanded veneer props from Marty Digmayer?

But for most projects or budgets hand-painting wood effect will remain the most viable and economic option. The first step is to spray the object, say a propeller, Matt White. Halfords White automotive primer is recommended for this and its fast drying time allows you to proceed quite quickly.

Using a slightly older brush with stiffer bristles, a mix of two parts artist's acrylic Raw Sienna to one part water is dragged over the propeller (do not have too much paint on the brush).

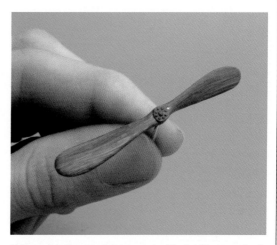

When dry, the work is repeated but with a coat of Burnt Sienna.

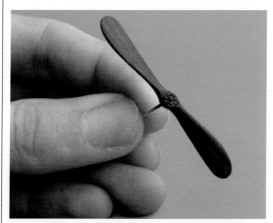

The penultimate coat consists of an application of Warm Sepia, otherwise known as Burnt Umber.

When completely dry, the work is finished off with a coat of Humbrol gloss enamel varnish for a wonderfully realistic mahogany propeller.

Wooden fixed-pitch airscrews are made from gluing laminations of certain woods together in a fan-like manner before sanding to shape; the most common woods used are walnut and mahogany, although birch and oak are used as well. As wood is not the most enduring of materials for such an occupation some wooden airscrews will be covered in a fabric or a cellulose covering, as well as with a brass leading edge and sheath over the tip to try to improve longevity. Consequently, not all wooden propellers will need to be painted to look like wood. Variable-pitch wooden propellers will certainly never be left bare as they are made of 'improved' wood, consisting of compressed birch impregnated with resin before being covered. The layered laminations of walnut and mahogany, each being about ¾ in thick, are clearly perceivable and can be painted accordingly. Other woods like spruce, as used for the interplane struts, have neither been glued to another type of wood nor have any perceivable grain of their own to try to represent.

CHAPTER 11

Moulds and Casting

At some stage in your hobby you will find yourself saying, 'If only I had some moulding equipment I could then cast my own parts!' In fact, going from the desire to the reality isn't that hard and with a basic understanding of how the materials for casting work you can be on your way in no time at all. This chapter in many ways relates to the chapters on scratchbuilding and conversion modelling, the most common requirement for casting your own parts being that you have laboured for hours to scratchbuild or significantly alter a kit part for which you will need duplicates. Taking this as the rationale for casting, the basic principle is to protect your sanity by reducing workload. Another rationale may be that you feel your scratchbuilding and cross-kitting work have left you with a potential aftermarket product. In such cases it is essential not to use the master, nor the first casting, but after that you can pour a cast for yourself and carry on with your own project. What happens to the master and first cast? The master is kept for taking more impressions should your product turn out to be successful, and your first cast is put away for emergencies.

There are dozens of very good companies selling hundreds of different silicones and resins. Most of them can be found using various search engines on the Internet, but a selection of companies has been included at the back of this book. It can all be a bit bewildering looking down the long lists of products, so the best thing to do is to find out if the company in question has an outlet in your country. If it

does, phone them up and ask to speak to a technician. Tell the technician exactly what you are trying to cast, including its basic measurements and volume. If you will be selling the parts then the colour of the resin may be an issue to you, as well as how fast the resin cures. Some products are more expensive than others and this may play a big part in your end selection – you really do get what you pay for with these products.

USING SILICONE

Silicone is measured in 'Shore'. The lower the Shore, the more flexible the silicone is. The most commonly used is 20 Shore, which is flexible enough to allow extraction of most resin casts without damage, but firm enough to keep its shape providing there is enough volume around the cavity. Another feature of silicone is how it cures. Silicone rubber can either be 'addition cure' or 'condensation cure'. Most of us are not that familiar with how various molecules react with each other under different circumstances and temperatures hence the need, as already advised, to speak to a technician before making a purchase. The addition-cure silicone is on average nearly double the price, so you need to know what you want. The key is shrinkage. The shrinkage factor in addition-cure silicones is almost imperceptible and that is why it costs so much. If what you are making isn't that big, or is just for yourself, you may be happy with a far cheaper silicone with a degree of shrinkage visible between the cast part and the master. If, however, your product is intended for the aftermarket, then you really do need a more expensive silicone – either that or you need to make your masters larger to compensate for the shrinkage caused by condensation-cured silicone. One more characteristic of silicone needs pointing out before we move on, which is that it is porous. Thus when you have demoulded your master from the mould, trace chemicals can be forced to the surface of the cavity and sometimes encourage air bubbles to stay put during casting. It is always good housekeeping to post-cure the mould in the oven for about four hours at 40°C.

USING POLYURETHANE RESIN

As for the polyurethane resin, two features need to be examined. Resin is graded by both how runny it is (viscosity) and by its pot life (the time you have to work with the material before it must be left alone) and cure time (the time the material takes to set). Again, as with the silicone, much depends on what you are casting and for whom. Resin that has a good deal of viscosity is certainly the most popular as it can seep into intricate mould detail much more easily; it also allows air to come up to the surface more readily. Much more important, however, is the other feature of resin – its cure time. The basic rule of thumb here is that the greater the cure time, the less shrinkage. Such resins, of course, cost more. In cheaper resins, the effects of shrinkage, caused by the much quicker exothermic reaction, can be markedly reduced by the addition of mineral filler. Up to 50 per cent mineral filler can be added to your resin mix, obviously reducing the amount of resin needed and thus the amount of heat generated by its faster cure time.

To sum up, where the part to be cast is thin or has marginal repercussions from any shrinkage, the cheaper condensation-cure silicone along with the cheaper fast-curing resin can be used. If, however, the part to be cast needs to be identical to the master, it is best to use the more expensive addition-cure silicone along with the more expensive slow-cure resin. Mineral filler can still be used, but its purpose changes to purely replacing expensive resin volume with inexpensive aluminium particles.

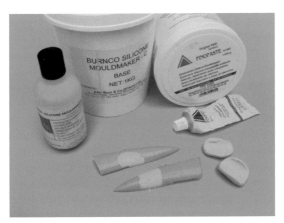

Silicone can be used to create an impression by pasting it onto kit detail in order to replicate a hatch or something. Silicone that cures fairly quickly is obviously better and putty needs to be used to back up the impression afterwards to keep the correct shape of the impression.

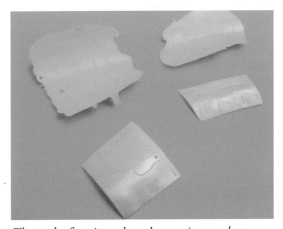

The result of pasting polyurethane resin onto the silicone impression, which, after trimming, gives you a nice set of new hatches that are much thinner than surgically removed kit parts.

The finished product! Tin or Lead foil work just as well but won't have the engraved detail that the silicone picks up – they can also be knocked out of shape, unlike their resin equivalents.

TOOLS

So much for the materials, what about the tools? An artist's spatula and inexpensive plastic measuring jug from a hardware shop are the obvious requirements for mixing silicone; a spatula is also needed for mixing the resin, plus a set of measuring spoons. What you mix it in depends on how much you are mixing. Small amounts can be mixed in small plastic photographic film canisters. Unused resin can be allowed simply to build up until you need to throw it away. Mixing larger amounts needs a more expensive option, such as a measuring jug. Fortunately, the plastic variety is normally flexible enough to allow the cracking and peeling off of surplus cured resin, leaving the measuring jug in good condition. Whatever you are mixing, it is of vital importance that you mix thoroughly and heed the mix ratios and stated pot life.

DEGASSING

For complicated or highly detailed moulds where air pockets are in abundance, you really do need a degassing chamber. This is obviously a major investment and not to be contemplated unless you are positive you will get the money back from making, and more importantly selling, many products. The degassing chamber works by evacuating the air from the chamber using a motorized pump. As the pressure gauge rises, so do the air bubbles abundant in the resin from mixing as well as the air trapped in the detail of the mould. Undercuts and sharp corners are notorious offenders! Equalizing the pressure and starting again (if the resin pot life permits) has the effect of jerking free any air pocket still resisting. The degassing chamber is also an excellent tool for making moulds that have a prolonged lifespan. Evacuating all the air from the silicone mix before it is poured on top of the master ensures that there will be few, if any, subterranean air pockets that might rip through after a few casts. Even if they don't rip through for a good few casts, you will know that they are there by having little dimples in your cast resin part. Be careful, however, when degassing silicone as it will rise considerably. For example, a mix of 150mil of silicone will easily reach the 400mil level before collapsing in on itself whilst degassing.

The need for a chamber can be avoided, however, by using slow-setting resin and slow-setting silicone. Using resin with a long cure time obviously gives greater pot life, which means you can attempt to take casts of more detailed parts and spend the extra time given by this kind of resin to burp, tap and prod the mould! Be aware that prodding around the inside of the mould to try to release trapped air pockets will eventually attack/erode the inner surface of the mould and thus limit its lifespan. The use of the slow-setting silicone ensures as much time as possible for the air bubbles to reach the surface and thus prevent many subterranean air pockets forming just under the surface of the cavity.

The other main tool that should be considered is the mould shell itself. The most accessible and simple tool in this case is probably Lego. The perimeter of the mould is bricked off and then back-filled with putty or tight-fitting plastic sheet on which to mount the master. The structure is then built up until it passes the top of the master by a couple of levels. One disadvantage of using Lego is that its joins are not airtight and so much slower-setting silicone can be lost, sometimes to the detriment of the project. One sure way to prevent this happening and make the clean-up operation easier is to line the inside of the Lego mould with Frisk Film.

VARIATIONS ON HOW TO MOULD

There are various ways to set about creating a mould. One method involves using silicone painted onto an area of plastic kit in order to take an impression of a particular panel. A faster-setting silicone is best for this and will need some putty laid over it when cured to give the impression of structural integrity. The brushed-on silicone picks up every bit of detail, a fact appreciated after resin has been brushed on a number of times until one has a sufficiently strong resin copy of the panel. A

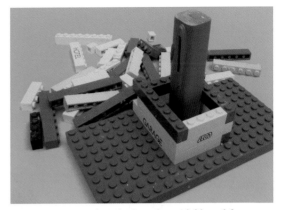

Lego is a very quick and relatively available tool for building small casting chambers. As the join lines in the bricks are not airtight it is best to line the inside of the chamber with products such as Frisk Film, which acts as a low-tack membrane. Here the master of a Ju 88 extended fuselage has been mounted onto card and the Lego is being built up around it (without Frisk Film in this instance).

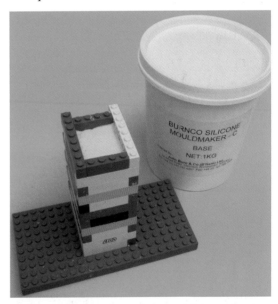

Making sure that you know the correct mixing and curing instructions for the silicone you are using, the mix is poured into the chamber. Without a vacuum chamber the mix will be full of air. If the silicone has a long pot life, you can afford to let the mix stand awhile for air to come to the surface. Painting the silicone onto the object to be cast as well as pouring as finely as possible into one corner of the chamber (away from the object) can help to decrease air bubbles in the mix.

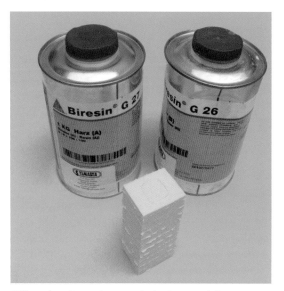

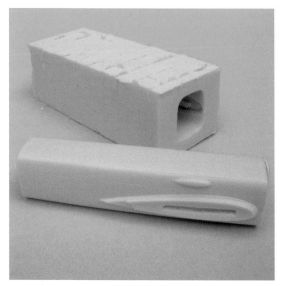

When the silicone has cured, the Lego and the master object can be removed and resin poured into the cavity mould. Again, be aware of how long you have to work with the resin and any other details such as recommended curing temperatures. Like the silicone, the resin mix will be full of air and more air will be trapped in sharp corners and overhangs when the resin is poured into the cavity mould. Without a vacuum chamber, burping, tapping and prodding the mould are the only answers to getting a quality bubble-free casting.

When the resin has cured, it can be manipulated out of the mould. Shown here is a 'flush' ended mould and the resultant casting. Masters with an additional casting or pouring block attached are better as you then have a definite line as to where to saw off the surplus resin and clean the part up. Without a vacuum chamber there will be more areas where air gets trapped. The master obviously also requires more resin as the one-piece pull mould will need to be longer in order to cover the object with the casting block attached.

The finished result – either a unique model for yourself or a potential aftermarket product – in this case my own AIMS conversion set to make the Italeri 1/72 Ju 88A-4 or A-16 into the extended fuselage Ju 88H-1.

new scalpel blade can then be used to cut back the resin part till you are left with a perfect replica of the kit's panel.

Even with the cheapest silicone and the cheapest resin you will find a great deal of satisfaction in being able to cast your own parts and thus add an extra dimension to your abilities to complete various scale aircraft projects. If scratchbuilding is *nostalgic*, then being able to make your own parts is surely *novel*.

Silicone moulds have a short casting life of about twenty casts. After this, the interior detail in the cavity mould will start to bond with the resin as shown here at the end of one of my Ju 88 weighted wheel mould's life. Bringing them into contact with white spirits or getting the resin mix wrong, or not shaking the canteens well before use so that the pour never cures properly, can speed up the decay of a mould further; the unstable chemicals in the resin will eat into the silicone mould and ruin it.

CHAPTER 12

Scribing

Scribing recessed panel detail is a slightly controversial subject, especially in 1/72 scale, as in reality you would not see recessed panel lines 72ft away from the real aircraft. At the most you might perceive tonal changes as the light bounced off irregularities in the fuselage skin. You would certainly not see rivet heads as perceivable sunken holes, but unfortunately this is an area where the competition winners have dictated what the standard should be so everyone else has toed the line. In defence of this practice it has to be remembered that there is an element to scale aircraft modelling that is inconsistent. We make things to scale but we do not view to scale! There is something entirely unrealistic about being able to stoop over a 1/72 aircraft model to judge it. The fact is that recessed panel lines in 1/72 scale simply look pleasing to the eye and help to break up uniformity. We might make to scale, but we view aesthetically. Whatever your opinion, recessed panel detail in the smaller scales is here to stay so let us look at how it is done.

TOOLS AND EQUIPMENT

Whether the need is to restore recessed panel detail that has been lost in the construction process (predominantly the area of the wing roots and fuselage spine), or to replace raised panel detail found on most older kits, a few simple tools and techniques will see you through. A number of companies produce very good tools designed to score the plastic and remove the unwanted waste at the same time.

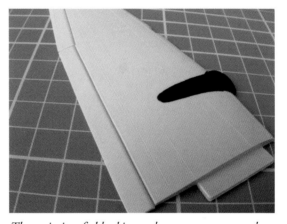

The majority of older kits, and even some more modern examples like Italeri's 1/72 Ju 88 range, come with raised detail. Whilst often crisp and very well represented, such raised detail is much less desirable than recessed panel detail, even though in 1/72 both styles are at fault where scale is concerned. The modeller therefore has to decide whether to delete the raised detail and replace it with paint-effect panelling or to try to rescribe at least the main construction seams without going too deep.

The most common is perhaps the P Cutter by Olfa, which comes in a number of different gauges. More slender products like the one from the Bare-Metal Foil Company can be very helpful where manoeuvrability is restricted. Other helpful tools include a good fine pencil and a number of different types of guide for the scribing blade to follow. Plastic credit cards are ideal for most straight lines as they are flexible enough to handle scribing across aerofoil sections, as well as being thick enough to offer a good guide. Where the curve of the kit part is too compound and where it would be helpful to have both hands free Dymo tape is excellent. Found in stationery shops, Dymo tape has sufficient tack to give you another hand free. Cut into much thinner lengths than designed for, it can cope with severe compound curves as well. The only danger to watch out for is that the tack is strong enough to pull up Milliput filler, so be extra careful when scribing in such areas. The final types of guide helpful in the scribing of recessed panel detail are templates. Eduard produce a number of these sets that are designed for the scribing of various inspection and fuel or oil filler hatches.

REMOVING RAISED PANEL DETAIL

Removing raised panel detail is harder than it sounds as it is apt to linger, requiring quite a thorough working over with various grades of wet and dry abrasive paper. A sanding block is helpful here as it aids uniformity in cutting back the plastic. Removing the raised detail completely, however, may not be totally advisable if, for instance, you then have no means of knowing where to scribe new panel detail. In such cases, those traces of former panel lines

that are so indefatigable may prove useful in guiding your hand later on. If, however, you have scale plans then it is always best to work from scratch and you can start laying out where new and revised panel lines should be with your pencil. Flexible plastic credit cards can help when taking up your pencil once more to join the basic layout markers together. Doing this on a grid square (like those found on cutting mats) will help to ensure that the panel lines are at the correct angles.

What you have just drawn can now be traced over with the scribing tool of your choice, using whatever guide is best for the occasion. Some scribing tools will cut heavier than others, so care is needed. In most cases, the work will involve taking a point furthest away from you and scribing back towards your body lightly for a number of passes. Scribing can be done away from the body as well, but for most people this feels unnatural and there is more risk of the scribing tool slipping away from the straight edge of the guide. A similar procedure is followed for the locating, drawing and then scribing of the kit's particular access panels. It is here that one more tool comes into play – the

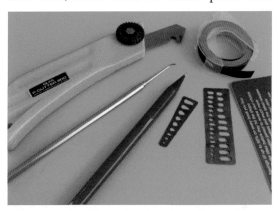

A selection of very helpful tools. Obviously a scribing instrument like the ones produced by Olfa and the Bare-Metal Foil Company is essential. What you use to guide the blade is up to you. Plastic credit cards and Dymo tape are worthy of consideration.

The first step is to remove any unwanted raised detail. Where the manufacturer has only included panel lines, and you are happy that they are in the right place, they can be removed by simply scribing over them; but where rivet detail is in abundance in company with the panel lines it is best to use a small sanding block and medium grit wet and dry abrasive paper to delete the unwanted detail.

Where plans are available the opportunity exists to lay out accurately where exactly you want to scribe the new detail, placing the kit parts over the plans so that the key features line up as closely as possible before the kit part is gradually withdrawn from the plans to expose where the main panel lines are. A mark can then be placed on the kit part where the scribing is to start.

Cord-wise panel lines running adjacent to the aircraft's central line are best drawn with the help of a grid. A straight edge is lined up both with the grid and the start point marked on previously and the line drawn where the panel will go.

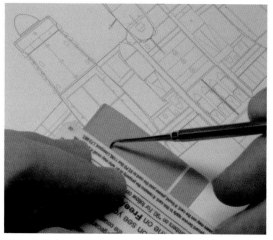

When all the cord-wise and span-wise panel lines have been marked, the work of scribing over them commences. On flat surfaces and on surfaces with a shallow aerofoil the straight edge of the old credit card will cope very well, enabling you to concentrate on scribing.

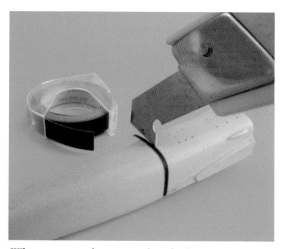

Where compound curves, such as fuselages, are concerned, however, you really need an edge that will adhere to the curve so that you have both hands free. Dymo tape is perfect for this when cut into thin strips.

pin vice. Having removed the head from a pin, secure the pin into a pin vice until within 3mm of its point. This sturdy little point is then scratched rather than scribed around the borders of the template design, be the work done in stages or in one pass without pausing.

There is no ability inherent in the pinhead to remove the plastic as with a scribing tool, so a number of passes needs to be performed just to get the scratched-in detail as clean as possible.

Another area where scratching is easier than scribing is in creating wheel tread detail. If you

Photo-etched brass templates are available for the scribing of more specific detail, though they are a little tricky to navigate scribing tools around.

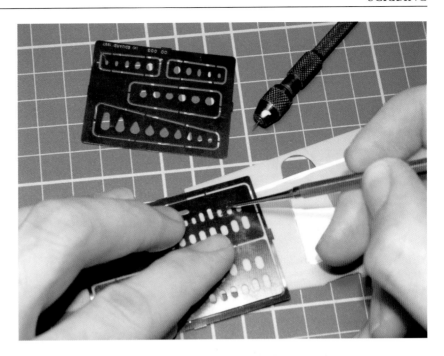

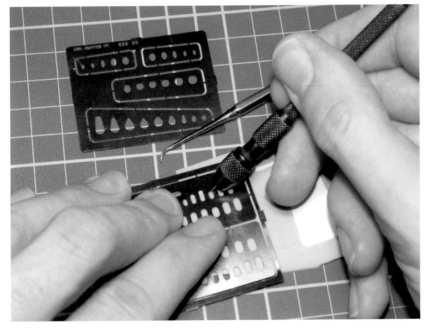

Another helpful tool is a deheaded pin, which can be secured into a pin vice and used to mark out detail. The pin drags rather than scribes but it has its uses.

have a hobby drill with a transformer that can get down to zero revolutions, then screw your wheel onto a drill bit. Hobby blades, like those from X-Acto, can be lined up together (but not glued) so that the two outer blades are just longer than the central blade. These are then placed in a vice, angled downwards to such an angle that they will come into contact with the slowly spinning wheel. As long as the revolutions are low, the wheel fixed securely to

A novel way of scribing wheel tread detail is to attach the wheel to the hobby drill using a drill bit. With the transformer on very low revolutions, the wheel is brought into contact with a number of new X-Acto blades angled down to meet it. Keeping the body of the hobby drill on the table will help to keep the pattern as tight as possible. Make sure that you wear safety goggles for this procedure.

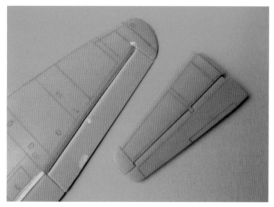

A helpful next step is to run diluted artist's black oil paint into the newly scribed detail. When the excess paint is wiped away with a cloth dampened with white spirit, leaving only the scribed detail with paint in it, one can clearly see where mistakes have been made and the appropriate remedial action can be taken. This step will also pick up where the scribing has been too shallow, as the damp cloth will have taken away the oil paint entirely.

spin without any oscillation, and the hobby drill firmly held in place, the blades will cut into the soft plastic of the kit wheel. Be patient and allow the blades to cut deeper and deeper into the plastic at their own pace; forcing the procedure will only splay out the outermost blades and thus disturb the pattern. Make sure to take adequate safety precautions when bringing spinning objects into contact with sharp objects.

With the scribing work done, a good way to check the accuracy of your work is to run into the recessed panel lines a wash of black artist's oil paint. This will help to highlight where you have not scribed deep enough as well as point out mistakes where you have perhaps slipped or held the guide at the wrong angle.

CHAPTER 13

Displaying Your Model

By Andrew Eaton

So having come this far you should now have a masterpiece ready to show off to your friends, family and fellow modellers, but before you go rushing out to your next club evening or model show it is worth giving some thought as to how you will display your model so that all your effort can be shown to its best effect. In particular, if you are going to enter your model into a competition some kind of a base to display it on is a must, as the way the model is presented will usually form part of the score it receives. Have a look through any of the reports from model shows that are published regularly in the monthly modelling magazines or on the Internet and you will see that almost without exception every model shown is on a base of some kind.

A look around the models on display at any model show will also reveal a multitude of different types of display bases ranging from plain pieces of coloured card to elaborate bases that take the model into the diorama category. It is not the intention here to cover any aspects of diorama making as it goes far beyond the scope of simply displaying the model and would need a whole book by itself to do justice to the subject. If this is something you wish to learn more about one of the best books covering the subject is *How to Build Dioramas* by Sheperd Paine (Kalmbach Books, 1980). A testimony to this book's usefulness is the fact that it is still in print over twenty years after first being published and covers all aspects of diorama making including painting figures. Dioramas can be impressive, but their intention

is to make the whole display into a single model and a great deal of time and effort therefore needs to be invested into the display as well as the model to have the desired effect.

For the majority of aircraft modellers it is the modelling of the aircraft itself that is the main attraction and the base is simply the means to present the piece without diverting the eye from the model. To give a sense of scale some modellers like to include a figure or piece of ground equipment on the base, and this is something usually allowed under most competition rules without moving the model into the diorama classes. Sometimes kits include standing pilot figures or ground equipment that can be included on the base; a good example of this is the tractor and bomb trolley included in the venerable Short Stirling kit from Airfix. Often these parts simply go straight from the kit box to the spares box, which is something of a shame as they are usually relevant to the model and therefore not only help to give some sense of scale, but also help to tell the viewer something about the aircraft itself.

One important factor to take into account with bases before you spend time making them is how you expect to use them. This may seem a fairly strange question as their use is obvious. However, if you only have a limited amount of space in which to display your models at home then having a separate base for each will cut down drastically the number of models you can have on show at any one time. If this is the situation, then the bases will probably spend most of their time in storage and only be used when models get taken to a club evening or show. In my own case, I have built a large display cabinet with several glass shelves in which I can comfortably display about fifty models of all shapes and sizes from a 1/72 scale B-52 down to a Polikarpov I-16. Lighting is provided solely from the room lighting, but as only a couple of the models are on bases enough light reaches the bottom shelf so that all models can be viewed properly. I have, however, over the last few years made a couple of dozen simple bases of different sizes and surfaces so that whichever type of aircraft I am currently modelling, whether it be a WWI biplane or a modern jet, I can normally find a suitable base on which to display it when I take it to my local model club. Since the method I have developed to make the bases is also fairly simple I know that if I do not have anything suitable then it will not take very long to make a new one.

TYPES OF BASES

As already mentioned, even straightforward display bases come in many shapes and sizes and with all sorts of materials being readily available at your nearest DIY store they are also very easy to make.

For the laziest amongst us the easiest option is simply to pick up a ready-made display base at the next model show you attend. For a couple of pounds you can buy a simple MDF

base all ready to display your model on. Some of these bases come ready covered in veneer of one type or another, whilst others are plain MDF and will therefore need covering and painting before they can be used.

One popular way of creating a simple base is to use a picture frame laid flat on the table with a suitable piece of wood, card or even mirror inlaid in the middle. While these sorts of bases are fairly cheap and certainly easy to make, they are to my mind unsatisfactory as the frame will always be higher than the inlay when the reverse is needed to display the model to its best advantage. They do, however, have the advantage that the inlay can be changed easily to represent different surfaces and a single frame can therefore be used for more than one base – though not at the same time.

My own preference is to make simple display bases out of MDF edged with iron on real wood veneer and with strips of wooden edging. MDF comes in sheets of various thicknesses, but for a display base a thickness of about 9mm is perfectly adequate for any size of base. Depending what your preferred modelling scale and subject matter is you should be able to get about a dozen bases from a single sheet of MDF. One useful tip is to plan beforehand what size of sheet you are going to buy and make a plan of how it should then be cut up to make the bases you require. All of the DIY stores have a timber cutting facility and for a small charge will be happy to cut up your large

Samples of the ready-made bases available at most model shows.

The basic materials for a simple base, MDF, iron-on veneer, edging strip and a piece of artist's board.

140

sheet into the required number of smaller pieces. Usually the most difficult part is trying to make them believe that it does not matter that the last piece will not quite be the width shown on the plan because a couple of mm of board is lost on each cut of the saw. Plan to use as few cuts as possible as normally you will be charged per cut. One big advantage of having the board cut there and then is that it is easier to transport it home cut into pieces on the back seat than strapped precariously to the roof or jammed into the boot. If you do decide to cut up the sheet yourself please remember that MDF dust should not be inhaled and a mask should be worn at all times when cutting it.

While you are buying the MDF other items you will need are the iron-on edging and some wooden edging strip. Unless you intend to paint the base instead of varnishing it try to match the type of wood in the veneer and edging, although a dark-colour varnish will hide small variations while still letting the wood grain show through so they do not have to be exact. The iron-on veneer is very easy to apply to the base and it should take no more than about ten minutes to cut and iron on the four strips around the top surface.

The wooden edging strips as found in DIY stores normally come in lengths of about 2m and it is very rare for a strip to be perfectly straight. When attaching it to the base it will therefore need holding in place somehow while the glue dries. The shape of it usually makes clamping it in place impossible and so the easiest way to hold it in place is either to use contact adhesive or a combination of double-sided tape and wood glue. One way this can be avoided is to use the iron-on edging on the sides of the base as well as round the edge of the top. This is what I have done with the base for the B-52 shown elsewhere in the book and the end result looks fine, although be prepared for some very awkward ironing. I suggest that if you prefer to do this you should use a thicker sheet of MDF to start with.

The reason I like to use the edging strip on most of my bases is that the profiled edge it gives to the base looks much better than the simple straight-cut edge of the MDF even if it is covered by the veneer. The most challenging aspect of the edging is to try to cut the ends at a consistent 45-degree angle so that they meet properly at the corners. Once the veneer and edging are on the base the gaps that you will inevitably have should be filled with some appropriately coloured wood filler, left to dry and sanded smooth. Once varnished, the presence of this filler even in large gaps at the corners will not be noticeable.

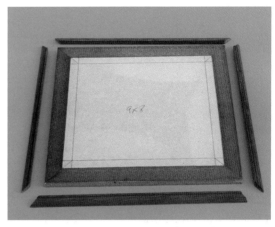

The base now has the wooden veneer ironed onto the top and is awaiting the attachment of the edging strips.

The edging strip has now been added, all gaps filled and sanded smooth. The artist's board has had the concrete grid drawn on with a black pen.

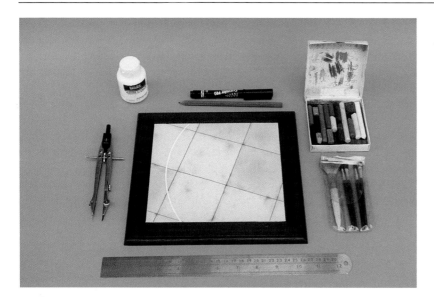

The completed base, with all of the weathering materials. The whole weathering process took no more than ten minutes.

A Fujimi Westland Lynx on the completed modern-style hardstanding.

FINISHING THE BASE

Having completed the base, attention can now be turned to the surface on which the model will be displayed. Depending on what sort of surface you want, this could range from a simple plain colour base, a mirror, concrete hardstanding, a carrier deck or some other surface. Specialized surfaces such as grass and water I will deal with later.

The most common sort of surface will be that representing an airfield hardstanding or runway and it is also very easy to replicate. The best medium for this is artist's board used for picture framing, which is available at most good art supply stores. It comes in large sheets in many colours and is also reasonably priced considering you should be able to do several bases from a single sheet. Even if you prefer to have a plain-coloured base artist's board is still a very good material as it is easy to cut and hardwearing enough not to get damaged under normal conditions. Artist's board also comes with either a smooth or slightly textured surface; for a concrete hardstanding the textured surface is ideal as it is a very good representation of the slightly ribbed finish sometimes found in

A section of tree trunk makes a very natural looking plinth for, say, a WWII Finnish subject in a forest clearing.

concrete. Colour is a matter of personal choice, but I have several sheets on hand in shades of sand and grey. One excellent reference source is the Osprey Publishing *Superbase* series of books published some years ago now, but all of which are filled with colour photos of various airbases throughout the world. These books not only help with choosing suitably coloured artist's board, but are also a good reference for the sort of markings that are found on runways or carrier decks.

Once you have your piece of suitably cut-to-size MDF the first step is to mark out the pattern for the concrete. Again, references are very useful here. Most Western airfields have a simple square pattern of various sizes, but in the old Warsaw Pact countries a hexagonal pattern was in use which may be more difficult to draw but is certainly different. First, mark out the lines in pencil with a ruler and then go over them in black pen freehand. You should end up with a basically straight but slightly uneven line. Again, it pays to study your references; some runways seem to have very neat lines of tar between the concrete sections while others have a very rough and ready finish. In addition there will often be repairs to concrete sections, so some squares will have black lines of tar

Samples of the excellent range of Osprey Publishing books that provide very good reference material for all types of base surface.

running thorough them. It is possible to give some depth to these lines by over-painting the pencil line with black paint instead of pen. This takes much longer and is difficult to do neatly but can be very effective.

Next, you should draw on any lines or other ground markings. Do not overdo this, as the area covered by the base represents only a small part of the overall airfield and so is very unlikely to be crowded with markings. Usually a simple line in either white or yellow will be more than sufficient. I find the easiest medium with which to paint the lines is acrylic paint as it is quick-drying and covers very well. I generally draw the line outline using ruler and compass in pencil and then paint the line in using a suitably sized brush. Masking off is unnecessary as this will give a too-perfect line.

The final task before attaching the artist's board to the base is to weather it. The easiest way to do this is with artist's pastels and a selection of soft brushes. Yet again, look at the references to see how weathering affects the real thing and then try to replicate this on the base. The aim is to try to give some depth to the flat surface of the artist's board. Subtle shading down the lines between concrete sections will do this and by using a large make-up brush and some dark pastel some of the sections can also be given a slightly different colour overall. Oil spills and other stains on the surface can be replicated with tiny spots of brown paint. The paper surface will act like blotting paper if the paint is thinned too much, so be sparing when doing this.

Like weathering on the model itself too much is very difficult to remove and can look unrealistic, so the golden rule is to stop before you think it is finished, have a break and then come back to it; more than likely it will look fine. When you are happy with the weathering the artist's board can be attached to the base.

ALTERNATIVE METHODS

If you are feeling adventurous there are alternatives to using artist's board. One very effective medium that can be used is sandpaper.

Depending on the size of the base this can either be applied as a single sheet and painted and weathered much the same way as the artist's board, or cut up and stuck on in individual squares. A very small gap should be left between the squares, which can later be painted with black paint. Sandpaper is not very easy to paint, but it does have two big advantages over artist's board. Firstly, by choosing a suitable grade of paper a very realistic textured surface can be obtained. This can be further enhanced by *not* using wet and dry paper, so that the surface can be textured even more by putting a couple of droplets of water on it (before painting), and using your finger to remove the sand in small areas. Once painted these worn areas are very convincing. The second advantage comes when you are applying oil stains. After painting, the sandpaper will not soak up thinned paint like the artist's board, so thinned enamel paint can be flicked and spotted onto the base to make some very convincing oil spills. The end result gives a much more three-dimensional result than artist's board but does take considerably longer.

Another alternative is to use the pre-printed Verlinden Productions airfield tarmac sections. Verlinden produce a series of four such sheets in 1/72 scale, two of which are concrete airfield sections, one a PSP (Perforated Steel Plating) section and lastly a modern aircraft carrier-deck section. All of these sheets are well done and can be used to produce some very versatile bases.

The Verlinden range of PSP, airfield and carrier-deck sections. These provide a good quick method of making a basic surface.

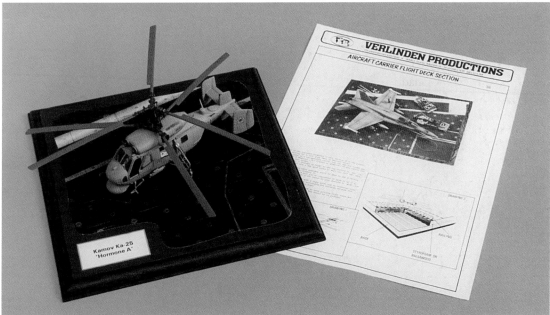

Examples of bases using the Verlinden range.

The two drawbacks with them are that firstly, despite some attempts by Verlinden to give depth by scouring and embossing, they still look rather picture-like and flat. Secondly, unless you want to have the sheets lined up anything other than square onto the base you will be limited to a small base area. When using these sheets I make the base in the usual way before attaching the Verlinden sheet onto a suitable piece of card and then attaching this to the base.

145

OTHER TYPES OF SURFACE

Of course, aircraft are not just restricted to airfield runways and hardstandings. Other common surfaces are grass, water, PSP plating and carrier decks. All of these surfaces can be reproduced fairly easily with good results.

For grass I have used two different methods depending on the size of the base to be made. For larger bases use grass matting roll as found in model railway shops. With this it is easy to cover large areas, but once attached it will need further work to take away the rather uniform bright green colour. Simple weathering with pastels and paint can quickly transform it into a much more lifelike grass field with a variety of plants growing amongst the grass. For smaller areas I generally cover the area in a thin but rough layer of plaster, let it dry before painting it an earthy colour and then use diluted PVA glue to cover the base in Verlinden static grass. Once dry, it can be dry-brushed or sprayed as before and even rubbed off in patches to let the earth underneath show through.

PSP plating has been used since WWII as a form of temporary airfield surface and as such is a useful type of base for anyone making models from any or all periods since WWII. Because of its uniform nature, however, the only practical way to do a base with this covering is to buy one of the commercially available products. Again depending on the size of base you require, there are several alternatives to use here. For small bases Eduard produce some excellent injection-moulded sheets of PSP plating in both 1/72 and 1/48 scales, a sheet of which will comfortably take a Phantom. If you have a lot of patience and money to spare you can buy photo-etched brass plating that has to be assembled much like the real thing. For larger surfaces the best option is to use the Verlinden sheets already mentioned.

The Eduard injection-moulded PSP sheet in 1/72. The sheet has been cut and repositioned to make it fit the shape of the plinth.

The types of grass base. On the left is grass matting used for railway layouts and on the right Verlinden static grass.

Carrier decks are often the scene of drama and excitement and can make an ideal background for models; compared to hardstanding, however, carrier decks are much more three-dimensional with all the tie-down points, catapult tracks, arrester gear and so on. As you would expect with all these features you can buy ready-made carrier-deck sections. Verlinden do their card rendition in the same series as their airfield sections and also some fine resin examples with raised exhaust deflectors. Given a little patience, however, it is perfectly possible to create your own carrier deck from a sheet of wet and dry abrasive paper and some Milliput. After covering the base with the wet and dry paper small depressions need to be drilled out in a regular pattern for the tie-down hooks. These can then be filled with Milliput and small sections carved out before it dries to leave a star shape. It is very difficult to be consistent with these tie-downs over even a small area, but with a bit of practice an acceptable result can be obtained so that when painted they look very convincing.

The last type of display base I shall mention is perhaps the most difficult to obtain a convincing result with . . . water. The likelihood with such a base is that any model displayed on it will have to be attached to it and it will effectively form part of the model. Every base will therefore be made for a specific model. Most models of float planes and flying boats come with some sort of beaching trolley or landing gear so that they can be displayed on a normal concrete hardstanding, but if you have the time and patience some very effective bases can be created that show off these types of aircraft to dramatic effect. Over the years I have made water bases with two different types of medium.

Firstly, for a real water effect clear, casting resin can be used. A quick look on the Internet will reveal a number of products suitable for use on bases, and most specialist craft stores will stock at least one of these. Working with these materials should be done with care as the fumes given off while the resin cures can be harmful. The Cessna model illustrated on page 149

A modern US carrier deck made using wet and dry abrasive paper with tie-downs made from Milliput.

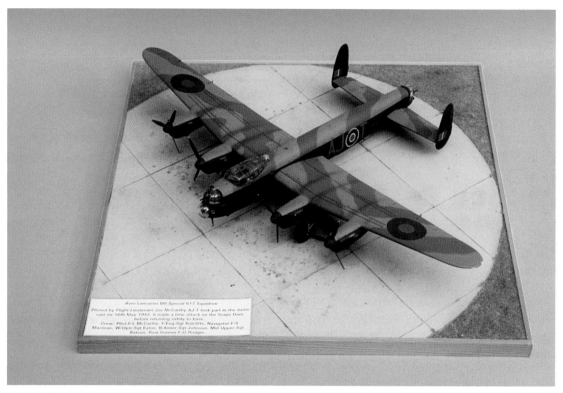

A typical WWII RAF base using individual squares of sandpaper and grass matting surround. Small tufts of static grass have been glued between the concrete sections and plenty of oil spills added under the engines.

was made a number of years ago and I cannot remember the manufacturer of the resin, but what clearly sticks in my memory is the door to the spare room being firmly shut with windows open for about a week whilst the resin hardened – every time I went to check on the base the whole house seemed to be infused with the smell. The garage would have been a better place to leave it had it not been winter and therefore too cold. Despite these drawbacks, clear casting resin gives excellent results. Depending on the make of resin used the top layer can be 'sculpted' with a hairdryer or toothpick to create ripples and avoid an unnaturally smooth surface. In the Cessna model I used bristles from an old paintbrush for the reeds and small pieces of green wool for weed in the water; the water lily leaves are circles of paper punched from a sheet of green colouring paper. The lily flowers themselves are

from some dried flowers we had in the house at the time and the pond weed is green paint stippled onto the surface of the cured resin. Over the years the resin has lifted very slightly from the base and there is some silvering underneath it similar to when decals are applied to a matt surface, but other than that the resin has proved very resilient to the effects of time.

The other way of making water is to use modelling clay of some description that can then be painted. This gives a much more solid feel to the base and is more suited to deeper water where you would not expect to see any sign of the bottom. The base for the Fairey Sea Fox shown opposite was made using Das modelling clay, and there are no waves except for the small variations in the surface made when smoothing out the clay with my fingers. The floats of the model were fixed to the base without the rest of the aircraft and the clay

Water – on the left using clear casting resin and on the right using Das modelling clay.

Close-up of the clear resin water with hole-punched lily pads. The detail in the water is a combination of green wool and slight silvering under the resin.

sculpted around them. Once the clay had set it was painted using artist's acrylic paints and given a couple of coats of acrylic gel to create a very slight rippled surface effect. A final couple of coats of Johnson's Clear were then applied to finish it off.

MAKING A DISPLAY CABINET

Displaying models should not just be about how you show them off to other modellers. Most of us not only enjoy making our models, but also displaying them at home when finished even if there is limited space in which to do so. Even if space is not at a premium the home has certain natural enemies to these delicate creations. Children, pets and dust all hold potential danger for models and the only way to avoid this is to display the models in some kind of display cabinet. I am fortunate enough to have the use of a room as a study with sufficient space to display the majority of my collection of completed kits. However, there were no commercially available display cabinets of the right size and shape, so I therefore took the plunge and constructed my own. The cabinet was designed with a minimum size in mind so that it would be able to display a 1/72 B-52 and a maximum size dictated by the room dimensions. All of the materials except glass shelves and perspex side panelling came from a local DIY store; the perspex was sourced from a specialist plastics supplier and the shelves from a local glazier.

Before I go any further I should say that I am by no means an expert carpenter and any close-quarter inspection will reveal that very quickly. The design of the cabinet was therefore kept as simple as possible and built using only the contents of a basic household tool box. I shall not go into too much detail of the construction other than to give a general description of how the frame was made up and stuck together. Essentially, the cabinet itself was made up of two pieces of plywood, one for the roof and one for the floor, connected at the corners by lengths of wood strip shaped in cross section like a cross with one-quarter filled in. This framework was then filled in at the back and one side with further sheets of plywood, leaving the front and other side for the perspex panels. Battens attached round the inside of the frame support the glass shelves. The front panel simply lifts out when access is needed to the interior of the cabinet. Underneath the display cabinet is another cabinet made in exactly the same way used for storage; the doors this time are off-the-shelf wooden panel doors. Construction overall took about three days at a cost of approximately £600 (mainly the glass shelves and perspex), but it has been well worth the investment.

I hope that this chapter has shown you that displaying your models properly is an important part of the overall process of modelling. What is more, the outlay in time and materials is very modest when compared to the actual kit. Enough material for several bases can be purchased for no more than the cost of a single kit and accessories, and can have as much an impact on the presentation of the final model as any amount of photo-etched brass or resin sets.

USEFUL ADDRESSES

TRADE ADDRESSES

Aeroclub
5 Silverwood Avenue
Ravenshead
Nottingham
NG15 9BJ
Tel: 0115 967 0044
Fax: 0115 967 1633

AIMS
32 Harvard Way
Amesbury
Salisbury
Wiltshire
SP4 7XE
Tel: 01980 622078
Email: j_s_mcillmurray@talk21.com
www.czechsixpublications.com

Cooper State Models
3245 E. Hillery Dr.
Phoenix
AZ 85032
USA
Tel: 602 867 8822
Email: copperst@amug.org
Fax: 602 867 1984
www.amug.org/-copperst/
For Marty Digmayer handmade props.

Hannants London
157–159 Colindale Avenue
London NW9 5HR
Tel: 0208 205 6697

Hannants Lowestoft
Harbour Road
Oulton Broad
Lowestoft
Suffolk

NR32 3LZ
Tel: 01502 517444
Fax: 01502 500521
www.hannants.co.uk

KingKit
Springhill Trading Estate
Aston Street
Shifnal
Shropshire
TF11 8DR
Tel: 01952 405020
Email: sales@kingkit.co.uk
www.kingkit.co.uk

Model Design Construction Ltd
Victoria Place
Victoria Road
Ripley
Derbyshire
DE5 4FW
Tel: 01773 513345
Email: models@modeldesignconstruction.com
www.modeldesignconstruction.com

Squadron Signal Publications
1115 Crowley Drive
Carrollton
TX
75011-5010
USA
Tel: 1 214 242 1485
Email: mailorder@squadron.com
www.squadron.com

EQUIPMENT TRADERS

Airbrush and Spray Centre Ltd
39 Littlehampton Road
Worthing
West Sussex

BN13 1QJ
Tel: 01903 266991
Email: enquiries@airbrushes.co.uk
www.airbrushes.co.uk
Retailers of the excellent Iwata airbrush and compressor range.

Cammett Ltd
Adlen House
Eardisland
Leominster
Herefordshire
HR6 9BD
Tel: 01544 388514
Fax: 01544 388514
Email: cammettco@btopenworld.com
Suppliers of such items as the Waldon Punch and Die Set.

The Daylight Company Ltd
89–91 Scrubs Lane
London
NW10 6QU
Tel: 020 8964 1200
Fax: 020 8964 1300
Manufacturers of an excellent range of powerful hobby lamps.

The Small Shop EU
Honeysuckle Cottage
Pound Lane
Gillingham
Dorset
SP8 4NP
Tel: 01747 825 646
Fax: 01747 825 646
Email: thesmallshopeu@aol.com
Manufacturers of such novel helps as the Hold & Fold tool as well as the Hair-Coat system.

Vacuum Equipment Services
Charles Square
Braggs Lane
Wrestlingworth
Sandy
Bedfordshire
SG19 2ER
Tel: 01767 631265
Fax: 01767 631265

M: 07831 559074
Retailers of degassing chambers for top-quality resin casting.

MOULDMAKING AND DESIGN CONTACTS

Axson UK Ltd
Unit 15
Studlands Park Industrial Estate
Newmarket
Suffolk
CB8 7AU
Tel: 01638 660062
Fax: 01638 665078
Email: sales@axson.co.uk
www.axson.com
For the very helpful mounting wax Plasticilin.

Bentley Chemicals Ltd
Rowland Way
Hoo Farm Industrial Estate
Kidderminster
Worcestershire
DY11 7RA
Tel: 01562 515121
Fax: 01562 515847
Email: info@bentleychemicals.co.uk
www.bentleychemicals.co.uk
For the excellent but expensive zero-shrinkage Rhodorsil RTV 4420 silicone and the excellent but expensive zero-shrinkage Smooth-Cast 325 polyurethane resin.

CMA Mouldform Limited
B6 The Seedbed Centre
100 Avenue Road
Birmingham
B7 4NT
Tel: 0121 333 5805
Fax: 0121 333 6010
Email: info@cmamouldform.co.uk
For resin casting.

MG Mouldings
7 Carnation Drive
Saffron Walden
Essex

CB10 2BE
Tel: 01799 500031
Email: mgmoulds@freenetname.co.uk
For resin and white-metal casting, photo-etched
brass and graphic designs.

Mouldlife
Packhorse End
Bridge Street
Moulton
Newmarket
CB8 8SP
Tel: 01638 750679
Fax: 01638 751779
For very reasonably priced silicones and moulds
including the silicone product **Tinsil 7020** (has
shrinkage factor) and the polyurethane resin **M10**
(has shrinkage factor).

John Burn
74 Albert Road
Stechford
Birmingham
B33 9AJ
Tel: 0121 508 4144
Fax: 0121 508 4145
Email: info@johnburn.co.uk
wwwjohnburn.co.uk
For a very flexible and not too expensive green
silicone with a small shrinkage factor.

Jon Freeman
25 Liberty Hill
Stannington
Sheffield
S6 5PU
Tel: 0114 2344744
Email: warhawk@blueyonder.co.uk
For reasonably priced decal design and layout
ready for silkscreen printing.

Precision Photofabrication Developments Ltd
Unit 3
Highbank Park
Lochgilphead
Argyll
PA31 8NN
Tel: 01546 602963
Fax: 01546 603029

For excellent and reasonably priced photo-etched
brass design and manufacture.

Sylmasta
Optum International
PO Box 262
Haywards Heath
West Sussex
RH16 3FR
Tel: 01444 415027
Fax: 01444 458606
Email: slymasta@aol.com
For a very nice resin for small quick jobs, you can
use the fast-curing G26 and G27 products (has
shrinkage). The G26B works very well with the
G27A. Sylmasta also sell Micromesh.

REFERENCE MATERIAL SOURCES

Albatros Productions Ltd
10 Long View
Chiltern Park Estate
Berkhamstead
Hertfordshire
HP4 1BY
Tel: 01442 875838
Fax: 01442 876018
Email: mail@windsockdatafilespecials.com
www.windsockdatafilespecials.com
Publishers of:
Windsock International
Bimonthly model magazine dedicated to
'stringbag' modelling with news, reviews, kit
builds and historical features.
Windsock Datafile series
Special look at the history of a particular
stringbag, or small family of such, with photos
and scale plans.

The Aviation Workshop Publications Ltd
Brook Barn
Letcombe Regis
Wantage
Oxfordshire
OX12 9SD
Publishers of:
On Target 'Profiles'
Purely artistic profiles of certain military aviation
subjects with great decal sheets by Model Alliance.

Axel Urbanke
Heckenkamp 24
26169 Bad Zwischenahn
Germany
Email: Axel-Urbanke@luftfahrtverlag-start
www.luftfahrtverlag-start.de
Publishers of:
Luftwaffe Im Focus
Fascinating bilingual collection of previously
unpublished colour and black and white
photographs of Luftwaffe subjects. (Sold in the
UK by Midland Counties.)

Greenhill Books
Park House
1 Russell Gardens
London
NW11 9NN
Publishers of:
Luftwaffe at War
An extensive series of photographic journals
illustrating the German Air Force on all fronts.

Guideline Publications
352 Selbourne Road
Luton
Bedfordshire
LU4 8NU
T:01582 505999
Publishers of:
Scale Aircraft Modeller
Monthly magazine featuring news, reviews, kit
builds and historical features.
Camouflage & Markings series and *Combat Colours*
series; both are rich in history, photographs and
artist profiles of military aviation subjects.

Hall Park Books
PO Box 1701
Milton Keynes
Buckinghamshire
MK17 8YZ
Tel: 01908 282292
Fax: 01908 282424
Email: hallpark@globalnet.co.uk
www.warpaint-books.com
Publishers of:
Warpaint Series
Highly valuable and affordable hardback

publications covering the paint schemes of
particular aircraft types, with historical narrative,
scale plans and short photo-essay.

Midland Counties Publications
4 Watling Drive
Hinckley
LE10 3EY
Tel: 01455 233747
Fax: 01455 233737
Email: midlandbooks@compuserve.com
www.midlandcountiessuperstore.com
Publishers of an extensive series of photographic
journals illustrating the German Air force on all
fronts.
Probably the largest retailers/publishers of military
aviation books such as the *Midland*, *Classic*,
Schiffer and *Hikoki* ranges of highly valuable, well-
illustrated, historical hardback books on various
military aircraft subjects. Also good for its
secondhand department to pick up such excellent
out of print titles as those in the Japanese bilingual
Aero Detail series.

Osprey Publishing
Elms Court
Chapel Way
Botley
Oxford
OX2 9LP
Email: info@ospreypublishing.com
Publishers of:
Osprey Aircraft of the Aces
Excellently informative references on the operation
history of a particular aircraft type and the men
that flew and did well in them. Also includes
inspiring colour profiles.
Osprey Combat Aircraft
Informative references, with colour profiles, of the
units that used non-pure-fighter type aircraft in
operations.
Osprey Modelling Manuals
Some of the biggest names in modelling show us
how to build excellent examples of a particular
aircraft type, with short photo-essay and other
helpful information.

Pol Models
64 Cumberland Road
Acton
London
W3 6EY
Tel: 02089 925106
M: 07887 886080
Email: Polmodels@aol.com
For Polish titles like the excellent *Monograph* series by AJ Press with scale plans and history and the *Wydawnictwo Militaria* series with factory plans and cutaways. Check whether what you want is available with English text.

Publications MBI
Czech-Six Publications
48 Station Road
Stoke D'Abernon
Cobham
Surrey
KT11 3BN
Tel: 01932 866426
Fax: 01932 867099
E-mail: mark@kmzchemicals.ltd.uk
www.czechsixpublications.com
UK outlet for publishers of many excellent bilingual military aircraft books.

SAM Publications
Media House
21 Kingsway
Bedford
MK42 9BJ
Tel: 08707 333737
Fax: 08707 333744
Email: mail@sampublications.com
Publishers of the excellent model aircraft magazines:

Scale Aviation Modeller International
Featuring news, reviews, kit builds and historical features
Model Aircraft Monthly
Dedicated to historical subjects.
Modellers Datafile series
Give in-depth looks into modelling a specific aircraft, with history, profiles, scale plans, reviews and photo-essays.

Squadron/Signal Publications
1115 Crowley Drive
Carrollton
Texas
75011-5010
USA
Tel: 1 214 242 1485
Email: mailorder@squadron.com
www.squadron.com
Publishers of:
In Detail & Scale
Details specific aircraft types noting their development with scale plans, profiles, photo-essay and reviews on models available at the time of print.
The excellent 'in action' historical development books and *Walk Around* photo-essay series of military aviation books.

4+ publications
Mark I Ltd
PO Box 10
100 31 Prague 10 – Strasnice
Czech Republic
Email: mark1@cmail.cz
Producers of excellent aircraft publications giving history, scale plans, profiles and photo-essays of the type at hand.

BIBLIOGRAPHY

The following books, articles and websites have been of great assistance to me in both the planning and writing of this book as well as the construction of the various builds therein. The help given by these sources has to be taken in tandem with the non-published help of many good friends who are much better at the various disciplines mentioned than I am and who were, and constantly are, willing to impart their vast experiential advice to me at the end of a phone, computer or over a cup of tea. I seriously recommend having three kinds of library, that which sits on your shelf until needed, that which exists in cyberspace and that which is alive and calls itself a model club.

BOOKS

Adams, J.W., *Vacform Modelling, A New Approach* (Aeroclub)
Adock, A., *F-15 Eagle in Action, Aircraft Number 183* (Squadron/Signal Publications)
Ashey, M., *Detailing Scale Model Aircraft* (Airlife Publishing Ltd)
   De Havilland Mosquito, Aero Detail, no. 23
Beaman, Jr, J.R., *Messerschmitt Bf 109 in action Part 2, Aircraft Number 57* (Squadron/Signal Publications)
Drendel, L., *Walk Around F-15 Eagle, Walk Around No. 28* (Squadron/Signal Publications)
Fearis, P.J., *The Samurai's Wings, Army, A Modeller's Guide to the Colour Schemes and Markings of Imperial Japanese Army Aircraft 1939–1945* (Peter J. Fearis)
Franks, R., *The de Havilland Mosquito, Modellers Datafile No. 1* (SAM Publications)
Gretzyngier, R. & Matusiak, W., *Osprey Aircraft of the Aces 21, Polish Aces of World War 2* (Osprey Publishing Ltd)
Griehl, M., *Junkers Ju 88, Star of the Luftwaffe* (Arms and Armour Press)
Hernandez, R. & Coughlin, G., *Osprey Modelling Manuals, Messerschmitt Bf 109* (Osprey Publishing Ltd)
Howe, S., *De Havilland Mosquito, An Illustrated History* (Crecy Publishing Ltd)
J2M3 Raiden. Koku (Fan book published by BURIN – DO., CO. Ltd)
Humphreys, R., *The Supermarine Spitfire, Modellers Datafile No. 3* (SAM Publications)
Merrick, K.A., *German Aircraft Interiors 1935–1945*, Vol. 1 (Monogram Aviation Publications)
Merrick, K.A. & Hitchcock, T.H., *The Official Monogram Painting Guide to German Aircraft 1935–1945* (Monogram Aviation Publications)
Ogilvy, D., *The Shuttleworth Collection*, (Airlife Publishing Ltd)
Price, A., *Spitfire, A Complete Fighting History* (Promotional Reprint Company)
Sakaida, H., *Imperial Japanese Navy Aces 1937–45, Osprey Aircraft of the Aces no. 22* (Osprey Publishing Ltd)
Stanton, M., *Scale Aircraft Modelling* (The Crowood Press)
Stenman, K. & Keskinen, K., *Finnish Aces of World War II, Osprey Aircraft of the Aces no. 23* (Osprey Publishing Ltd)
Trojca, W., 'Junkers Ju 88', *Model Hobby* (Vol. 1)
Verlinden, F., *On Plastic Wings, The Verlinden Way*, Vol. III (Verlinden Publications)

ARTICLES

Beyts, H., 'Tools & Techniques, Rigging', *Scale Aircraft Modelling* (Vol. 22, No. 9, November 2000)
Edwards, J., 'Tools & Techniques, Rigging – The Wind in the Wires', *Scale Aircraft Modelling* (Vol. 19, No. 8, October 1997)

Sekularac, A., 'Revolutionary "Rat" Polikarpov 1-16 Early Type 5', *Scale Aircraft Modelling* (Vol. 26, No. 4, June 2004)

Wigman N., 'Grumman's Bent Wing Bird', *Scale Aviation Modeller* (Vol. 10, Issue 8, August 2004)

WEBSITES

Aungst, D., 'Custom Decals', an article for Hyperscale.com

Benolkin, M., 'Make Your Own Inkjet Printer Decals', an article for internetmodeler.com

F-15E Strike Eagle.com

Green, B., 'Why Build a Vacform Model?', an article for Hyperscale.com

Kerr, J., 'Natural Metal', an article for Hyperscale.com

Index